Michael English

The
Ha'penny
Bridge

Dublin

Comhairle Cathrach
Bhaile Átha Cliath
Dublin City Council

with special contributions by

Michael B. Barry

Annette Black

David de Haan

Seán Harrington

Michael Phillips

Logan Sisley

Gerard Smyth

For my sons Daniel and Tom and my nieces Matilda, Abby and Isabel.

First published in 2016 by Dublin City Council

Dublin City Library & Archive,
138 - 144 Pearse Street,
Dublin.
D02 HE37

ISBN: 978-1-907002-22-9 Hardback

ISBN: 978-1-907002-29-8 Paperback

Comhairle Cathrach
Bhaile Átha Cliath
Dublin City Council

Funding for this book was provided by Dublin City Council.

Design and typesetting by Black Mountain Design, Dublin.

Printed in Ireland by Print Media Services, Dublin.

Photography by Michael English.

Additional photographic material supplied by organisations, companies and individuals is credited on the relevant pages.

Contents

This page

Ha'penny Bridge

Drawing in pencil - 1950
Artist unknown
Courtesy of Dublin City Council

Following pages
in order of appearance

The bridge at high tide

Photograph by the Author

**Ha'penny Bridge,
Dublin**

Oil on canvas - 2000
61 x 76 cm
by **Brian Ballard**
Courtesy of the Artist

**Reflected structure
on a winter tide**

Photograph by the Author

**Ha'penny Bridge,
Winter Evening**

Acrylic on canvas - 2007
Size 65 x 45 cm
by **David Farren**
Courtesy of the Artist

Coin actual size

**The Hibernia
Half Penny Coin**

This was the coin
that lent its name
to the current
structure. The
bridge was tolled
and pedestrians
wishing to cross it
were each charged
a half penny.

While the bridge
had a number of
official names this
was the one which
resonates with
Dubliners to this
day.

See also page 67

0   page 23

Introduction
An engineer's perspective
by Michael Phillips

3   page 85

The Bridge under Threat
Hugh Lane's vision for Dublin
by Logan Sisley

6   page 183

A new Lease of Life
The structure and its restoration
by Michael B. Barry

1

page 33

Coalbrookdale, England
The genesis of industrialisation

by David de Haan

2

page 61

Distinctly Pedestrian
The history of the Ha'penny Bridge

by Gerard Smyth

4

page 119

The Pint of Plain
Shipping the black stuff overseas

by Michael English

5

page 153

Cultural Awareness
Part of Dublin's cultural quarter

by Annette Black

7

page 213

Marking the Millennium
A tale of two bridges

by Seán Harrington

8

page 238

Night into Day into Night
Capturing the climatic variations

by Michael English

11

1815
Work begins on Ha'penny Bridge

1816
Ha'penny Bridge opens and is named *Wellington Bridge* in honour of the Duke's victory over Napoleon

1819
Simón Bolívar liberates Colombia, Venezuela and Ecuador from Spain

1820
Discovery of Antarctica

1823
Catholic Association formed by Daniel O'Connell

1815
Congress of Vienna convened and redraws the map of Europe at the end of the Napoleonic Wars
Napoleon flees exile and is finally defeated at Waterloo

1815
Mount Tambora in Indonesia erupts in the largest volcanic emission in recorded history. It creates a climate known as the *Volcanic Winter* in Europe during the summer of 1816

1831
Belgium secedes from the Netherlands

1832
Irish Reform Act allows greater representation in London Parliament

1833
Slavery abolished in British Empire

1834
Ireland's first Railway opens Dublin - Kingstown
Spanish Inquisition officialy ends

1836
Royal Irish Constabulary formed
Colt patents the revolver

1837
Telegraphy patented by Morse

1824
Beethoven's 9th Symphony

1826
Niépce pioneers photography
Internal combustion engine patented

1829
Catholic Relief Act passed to allow Catholics to sit in Westminister Parliament.
Greece gains independence from Turkey
First electric motor built

1845
The Great Famine begins

1847
Death of O'Connell
Brontës publish *Jane Eyre & Wuthering Heights*

1848
United Irishmen newspaper published
California Gold Rush
Marx & Engels publish *The Communist Manifesto*

1849
Safety pin and gas mask invented

1850s
Revival of Protestant *Evangelicalism* in Ulster and the rise of *Fenianism* in the south lead to a more politicised society

1853
Crimean War starts

1855
Bessemer process allows mass production of steel

1840
Province of Canada established and New Zealand founded

1843
The Harp is adopted as the national symbol of Ireland
O'Connell holds *'Monster Meetings'* to repeal the Act of Union of 1800

1856
Neanderthal Man is identified

1857
'Phonautograph' invented to record sound

1859
Unification of Italy commences

1861
American Civil War begins
Russian serfs emancipated

1863
Formation of International Red Cross leads to first Geneva Convention

1865
Pasteur patent's milk and beer pasteurization

1866
Austro-Prussian War
Nobel invents dynamite

1867
Fenian Rising by Irish Republican Brotherhood

1869
Charles Stewart Parnell enters politics
Suez Canal opens
Tolstoy publishes *War and Peace*

1870s
Belfast named Linen Capital of the world

1873
Blue jeans and barbed wire invented

1874
The Impressionists hold their first exhibition in Paris

1876
Bell invents the telephone

1879
Michael Davitt founds *The Land League*
Edison invents electric light

1883
Krakatoa Volcanic explosion

1884
The GAA is founded
Maxim invents the machine gun

1885
Parnell's Irish Party gains in election forcing Parliament to endorse Home Rule question

1886
1st Irish Home Rule Bill is defeated

1887
Dunlop pioneers pneumatic road tyres

1889
Eiffel Tower erected
Aspirin patented

1891
Death of Parnell

1893
2nd Irish Home Rule Bill passed in Commons but rejected by the Lords
New Zealand is first country to grant women the vote

1895
X-rays discovered by Roentgen.
Lumière brothers premiere motion pictures in Paris

1896
First modern Olympics are held in Greece
Marconi's first public wireless transmission

1897
Bram Stoker publishes *Dracula*

1898
The Curies discover rad and poloniu

1899
2nd Boer South Afri

1903
Wrigh broth fly firs power aircraf
Teddy inven

Einstei theory relativ

Fe sta m assem of c

The Ha'penny

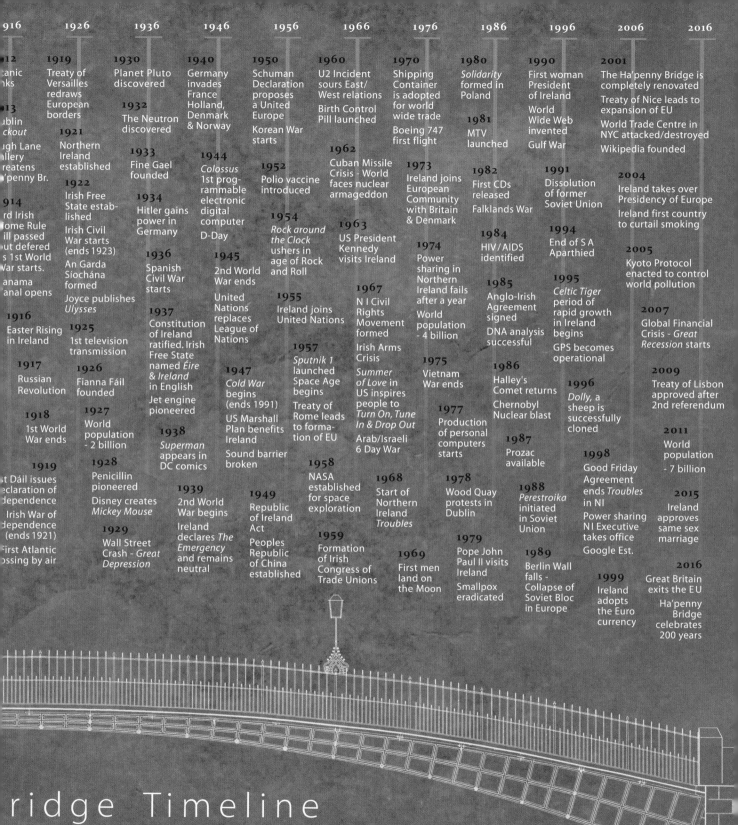

1912
Titanic sinks

1913
Dublin lockout

Hugh Lane Gallery threatens Ha'penny Br.

1914
3rd Irish Home Rule Bill passed but defered as 1st World War starts.

Panama Canal opens

1916
Easter Rising in Ireland

1917
Russian Revolution

1918
1st World War ends

1919
1st Dáil issues Declaration of Independence

Irish War of Independence (ends 1921)

First Atlantic crossing by air

1919
Treaty of Versailles redraws European borders

1921
Northern Ireland established

1922
Irish Free State established

Irish Civil War starts (ends 1923)

An Garda Síochána formed

Joyce publishes *Ulysses*

1925
1st television transmission

1926
Fianna Fáil founded

1927
World population - 2 billion

1928
Penicillin pioneered

Disney creates *Mickey Mouse*

1929
Wall Street Crash - *Great Depression*

1930
Planet Pluto discovered

1932
The Neutron discovered

1933
Fine Gael founded

1934
Hitler gains power in Germany

1936
Spanish Civil War starts

1937
Constitution of Ireland ratified. Irish Free State named *Éire* & *Ireland* in English

1938
Superman appears in DC comics

1939
2nd World War begins

Ireland declares *The Emergency* and remains neutral

1940
Germany invades France Holland, Denmark & Norway

1944
Colossus 1st programmable electronic digital computer

D-Day

1945
2nd World War ends

United Nations replaces League of Nations

1947
Cold War begins (ends 1991)

Jet engine pioneered

US Marshall Plan benefits Ireland

Sound barrier broken

1949
Republic of Ireland Act

Peoples Republic of China established

1950
Schuman Declaration proposes a United Europe

Korean War starts

1952
Polio vaccine introduced

1954
Rock around the Clock ushers in age of Rock and Roll

1955
Ireland joins United Nations

1957
Sputnik 1 launched Space Age begins

Treaty of Rome leads to formation of EU

1958
NASA established for space exploration

1959
Formation of Irish Congress of Trade Unions

1960
U2 Incident sours East/West relations

Birth Control Pill launched

1962
Cuban Missile Crisis - World faces nuclear armageddon

1963
US President Kennedy visits Ireland

1967
N I Civil Rights Movement formed

Irish Arms Crisis

Summer of Love in US inspires people to *Turn On, Tune In & Drop Out*

Arab/Israeli 6 Day War

1968
Start of Northern Ireland *Troubles*

1969
First men land on the Moon

1970
Shipping Container is adopted for world wide trade

Boeing 747 first flight

1973
Ireland joins European Community with Britain & Denmark

1974
Power sharing in Northern Ireland fails after a year

World population - 4 billion

1975
Vietnam War ends

1977
Production of personal computers starts

1978
Wood Quay protests in Dublin

1979
Pope John Paul II visits Ireland

Smallpox eradicated

1980
Solidarity formed in Poland

1981
MTV launched

1982
First CDs released

Falklands War

1984
HIV/AIDS identified

1985
Anglo-Irish Agreement signed

DNA analysis successful

1986
Halley's Comet returns

Chernobyl Nuclear blast

1987
Prozac available

1988
Perestroika initiated in Soviet Union

1989
Berlin Wall falls - Collapse of Soviet Bloc in Europe

1990
First woman President of Ireland

World Wide Web invented

Gulf War

1991
Dissolution of former Soviet Union

1994
End of S A Apartheid

1995
Celtic Tiger period of rapid growth in Ireland begins

GPS becomes operational

1996
Dolly, a sheep is successfully cloned

1998
Good Friday Agreement ends *Troubles* in NI

Power sharing NI Executive takes office

Google Est.

1999
Ireland adopts the Euro currency

2001
The Ha'penny Bridge is completely renovated

Treaty of Nice leads to expansion of EU

World Trade Centre in NYC attacked/destroyed

Wikipedia founded

2004
Ireland takes over Presidency of Europe

Ireland first country to curtail smoking

2005
Kyoto Protocol enacted to control world pollution

2007
Global Financial Crisis - *Great Recession* starts

2009
Treaty of Lisbon approved after 2nd referendum

2011
World population - 7 billion

2015
Ireland approves same sex marriage

2016
Great Britain exits the EU

Ha'penny Bridge celebrates 200 years

...ridge Timeline

Introduction

by Michael Phillips

Former City Engineer, Dublin City Council

T he building of bridges across urban rivers is an integral part of a city's or town's growth down through the centuries. The pace and number are determined both by the demand from communities living on both sides of the river and also by the economic activity occurring at those periods of time. The replacement of a ferry or ford crossing by a bridge immediately eliminates both the danger of drowning and the fear felt by families while waiting for their 'loved' ones, who have to cross the river, to return home.

The substitution of the Bagnio Slip ferry with the Ha'penny Bridge is an example, which is repeated in modern day society, where a completely new way of achieving something beneficial to the community is only allowed on a temporary basis and with conditions. And so it was that the municipal authority, Dublin Corporation, held power of veto over the bridge. This was possibly due to a fear of the new material proposed – iron - and also the fear that the Corporation might be liable for costs if the new bridge was not successful. However, the promoters of the bridge were confident that it would make money. Their view was formed even with the completion of the original O'Connell Bridge (then Carlisle Bridge) in 1794 downriver of the proposed location which had plenty of

Opposite

The Ha'penny Bridge in the early 1950s
Courtesy of Dublin City Council

23

space for pedestrians. In addition the citizens of Dublin regularly witnessed the collapse of an arch in the existing bridges as a result of storms and flood surges in the river. In not charging tolls for the initial ten days the developers assisted in overcoming such concerns.

The structure there today forms a critical part of the initial phase of the Industrial Revolution because most metals in use today evolved either from the material or the process used in the Ha'penny Bridge. This is particularly obvious if you stand on the bridge and witness its structure, which is predominantly metal.

The collection of essays in the book tells the story of the bridge both from a construction and a social aspect. This is welcomed because the role the bridge was to play in society at the time becomes very apparent and it brings the story of the bridge to life. We tend to think of bridges and other infrastructure in the context of today's needs and when Dublin City Council decided to refurbish the bridge in 2001 it was because we were aware that the bridge was as relevant in our time as it was when it was built. In fact the Ha'penny bridge is what identifies Dublin in photographs along the river in the city centre. In addition its popularity is highlighted by the fact that it is the only bridge where the practice of fixing *'love locks'* occurs. While this practice can damage parts of the bridge it does give it international recognition and the public are claiming it as their own.

In recent years the public have taken a very active interest in the history of the bridges in Dublin, particularly those over the River Liffey. As a result the City Council created a website *www.bridgesofdublin.ie* and published a book *Bridges of Dublin* to further facilitate and promote the engineering history of Dublin. This book by Michael English, which focuses on a particular favourite bridge of the public, will greatly enhance the information and knowledge available and the Council is delighted to be publishing it.

Michael Phillips

Former City Engineer

Opposite

The Ha'penny Bridge

Oils on canvas - 2009
40 x 35cm

by **Tom Byrne**

Courtesy of the Artist

Following pages

**A Bird's Eye View
of Dublin**

Published by *The Graphic*
27 December 1890

Engraving

by **H W Brewer**

An aerial view of the city with the Ha'penny Bridge, now 74 years old in view. It was very probably drawn from the vantage point of John's Lane Church steeple in the foreground.

Courtesy of Dublin City Council

H.W.Brewer 1890.

Horizon	Malahide	Donaghmede	Lambay Island Sutton	Fairview Fairview Viaduct	Clontarf	Hill of Howth *very exaggerated*		Bull Island
Background	Parnell Square	Mountjoy Square	Nelson's Pillar *replaced by Spire* Jervis Street Hospital	The Five Lamps	Amiens Street Rail Station	O'Connell Bridge	Custom House Dublin Port	Trinity Colleg
Central	The Four Courts Inns Quay	Capel Street	Richmond Bridge *now O'Donovan Rossa Bridge*	Grattan Bridge	Ha'penny Bridge Wood Quay	Temple Bar	Dame St. City Hall	Christ Chur Cathedra Synod Ha
Foreground	Merchants Quay Bridge Street		The Church of Adam & Eve		St. Audeon's & St. Audeon's Catholic Church *(behind)*			High Street

IEW OF DUBLIN

BREWER 1890

All locations are approximate

...ley ...htouse	Great South Wall	Poolbeg	Dublin Bay		Kingstown Harbour		Kingstown *now Dun Laoghaire*		Killiney Hill Blackrock Village
...ingsend ...nd Canal Basin		Irishtown		Sandymount Strand	Merrion Strand		Ballsbridge		Ranelagh Donnybrook
...nt ...drew's ...rch	Dublin Castle	St. Werburgh's Church	Grafton Street	Leinster House, Nat. Library & Museum	Whitefriar St. Church	St. Stephen's Green Merrion Square		Portobello	Saint Patrick's Cathedral
	Back Lane	Tailor's Hall	John's Lane Church & Steeple			Francis Street	St. Nicholas of Myra Church		The Liberties

The Halfpenny Bridge

by Niall O'Connor

Georgian iron and treacherous timbers,
slime covered and slippery up and down;
a pox on the ferryman's earnings
by those who dare to cross
from mean street to Venetian passage,
this is the Ha'penny bridge

Leaning on both North and South,
owned by neither, both,
a no-man's land
twixt Norse and Brit,
chained to the granite quays.

On its crest
its pinnacle,
the luckless Lord Mayor of Dublin;
the toll gatherer-beggar,
with his bowl forever sits,
selling poverty for a pittance,
and redemption for avoiding eyes

The royal barge,
the chieftains byre,
bananas from Bolivia,
they all have passed
beneath this throne,
this crown of Anna Livia.

From the collection *Change in the Wind*
by Niall O'Connor

Following pages

A View of the Upper Works at Coalbrookdale, in the County of Salop.

Engraving - 1758

by **Francis Vivares**

Published by G. Perry and T. Smith 1758, according to an Act of Parliament.

Image copyright and courtesy of the Ironbridge Gorge Museum Trust

Coalbrookdale
England

The genesis of industrialisation

1

The genesis of industrialisation

by David de Haan

Director of the Ironbridge Institute, retired

he Ironbridge Gorge in Shropshire, England is about 56 kilometers northwest of Birmingham, in a beautiful wooded valley which at first sight today offers few clues to its past. Yet by 1800, when the Gorge was known as Coalbrookdale, it was the most industrialised area in the world and proved fascinating for artists eager to capture the theatre of fire and smoke that filled the skies. They saw drama, power and excitement, positive terms that describe what we would recognise today more negatively as pollution, but that is a much more recent concept and not one they would have recognised. In reality life expectancy in this polluting environment was low. The ironmaster Abraham Darby I died aged 39, his son Abraham II fared better at 52, but his grandson (the builder of the Iron Bridge) died at 38.

We need to go back about 12,000 years to the last Ice Age to understand why industry developed around Coalbrookdale. As the climate warmed up, melting water was trapped between the slowly receding ice cap to the north and a ridge of hills to the south, building up a large lake. But it cut an escape route and so carved the 100 metre-deep valley through which the River Severn now flows, exposing the raw material on the valley

Opposite

The inside of a Smelting House, at Broseley, Shropshire

Engraving - 1788

by **G. Robertson**

Published February 1788, by John & Josiah Boydell. Cheapside, London.

Once a furnace reached the working temperature it would operate day and night, week after week for up to six months. Here, workers guide the flaming, molten iron down into the waiting moulds.

Working in a blast furnace was extremely dangerous with little in the way of safety or protection. The extreme heat lead to acute exhaustion and loss of concentration which often resulted in serious injury or even death.

Copyright and courtesy of the Ironbridge George Museum Trust

Above

Eye-patch box

Ironbridge souvenir

Photograph courtesy of Robert Morrissey

sides. No one had to guess what minerals were to be found. From early times it was evident that limestone, coal, iron ore and clay were there in abundance and could be extracted from tunnels driven into the hillside. Nature had also conveniently provided a transportation route at the valley bottom in the form of the river. It is therefore no surprise the Severn Gorge was to become an industrial area. Limestone was extracted in early medieval times; there was coal mining since 1332 and ironstone mining began in the 15th century with much of the coal being shipped down by river. Ironmaking started a little later, with reference to a smithy forging blooms in Coalbrookdale by 1536, and steelmaking from 1619. This was on a relatively small scale, as in 1700 the 'whole village consisted of only one furnace, five dwelling houses, and a forge or two'. The real growth came, soon after the beginning of the 18th century when new technology made cheap iron a possibility.

Alternatives to charcoal had been actively sought for furnace industries since at least 1615 when a royal decree by King James I aimed at glassmakers demanded that coal be used as an alternative. However, for ironmaking the sulphur in coal made the direct substitution unworkable, but experiments with coal converted to coke were to prove the solution. Around 1700 several people tried to make iron with coal or coke, including Sir Clement Clerke and Shadrach Fox. However, credit for perfecting the process goes to the Quaker ironmaster Abraham Darby I (1678-1717) who succeeded in making good quality coke-smelted iron at Coalbrookdale in 1709, largely due to the particular type of local coal which was very low in sulphur. This *'clod coal'* was ideal for converting to coke. While not yet suitable for making wrought iron, the materials worked perfectly together to produce a strong free-flowing metal, ideal for casting into thin-walled cooking pots. At about half the thickness of charcoal iron pots, they were lighter to handle and Darby could make more products from the same amount of iron.

Below
Ironworks at Snedshill
Engraving - 1820
by **Francis Nicholson**
Printed by C. Hullmandel

J.N. 1820.

near Shiffnall.

The process required roasting heaps of coal covered in turf over 36 hours which, in the absence of air was converted to coke. This is exactly the same process whereby wood is converted to charcoal. Iron ore was also roasted slowly over several days and was then fed in the top of the blast furnace by the barrow load or basket, along with coke and limestone in the proportions of twelve baskets of iron ore to three of limestone and

Contrast this vivid industrial scene by Nicholson (above) with examples by Smythe, (opposite) and by Vivares on pages 30/31.

This is a much more realistic rendition of a region beset with the worst and most acute, pollution in the world.

35

nine of coke. Bellows kept the temperature up and as the iron ore melted it would trickle down to the bottom of the furnace where it could be tapped off every four hours. Impurities in the ore mixed with the limestone to form a scum on top of the iron, which could be tapped off separately. The first *'charge'* of iron ore put in the top of the furnace would be converted to molten iron about six metres below in about 44 hours, but once going the furnace was continuously charged and would stay in opera-tion for about six months before the brick lining had to be repaired. Each tapping of the furnace produced about four tons of iron.

Freed from the constraints of coppicing woodlands for charcoal, coke-fired furnaces could be grouped close together. Such was the demand for iron that Darby was able to construct a second furnace at the other end of the ironworks in 1715 and in the 1750s furnaces were usually built in pairs. However, a charcoal-fired blast furnace needed around four square miles of managed hard woods – especially hornbeam, hazel and blackthorn, rather than beech or oak which did not re-sprout in the same way – to support its demand for fuel, so the next nearest *charcoal* blast furnace was likely to be at least over six kilometres away. Claims that the furnacemen decimated the forests are untrue because they would only take wood from every 20th coppiced tree so the crop could continue to regrow. The decimation of the forests came from the ship and house builders who cut down the larger trees, ones that would take 200 years to grow.

This happy coincidence of ideal raw materials found in Coalbrookdale was not true elsewhere, so in effect Darby's company had a monopoly on cheap cast iron for many years. The result was an increase in sales, and the profits from cooking pots and kettles allowed the Coalbrookdale ironworks to explore new uses for

cast iron – starting with wheels in 1723, steam engine cylinders in 1729, iron rails in 1767 and the Iron Bridge in 1779. However, the coke iron was not initially suitable to converting to wrought iron, which was where the big demand lay. It took about 40 years of experimenting in Coalbrookdale by Darby's successors, particularly Richard Ford and Abraham Darby II (1711 - 1763), until the process became reliable and cheaper than charcoal smelting. Once successful the new demand led to the building of nine new coke blast furnaces in the region between 1750 and 1760.

One of the most informative images of the Coalbrookdale works is from 1758 engraved by Francis Vivares (see chapter start) which shows a large cast iron cylinder being hauled by a team of horses past the blast furnaces. Like so many industrial scenes, it reveals the influence of the promoter once the full story is known. Art as evidence is always suspect. So often the true nature of the hardship, the pollution and the industrial squalor is ignored, cleaned up, or even glorified. This engraving is no exception. It shows the rural landscape around the Coalbrookdale works, the iron-masters' houses, workers' terraces, and discreet puffs of smoke rising from a few chimneys – yet it was a successful ironworks, which at the time was the largest ironmaking company in the world with 500 employees. The scene is still recognisable because remarkably most of the buildings survive to this day and cast iron products are still being made on the same spot after 300 years of continuous production. The steam engine cylinder in the foreground was selected to demonstrate how up-to-date their products were and to remind the viewer of the company's technological supremacy. The picture shows a tranquil scene, but the reason for

commissioning the view was more sinister. They were in trouble and fighting a court case for survival. Their rival ironmaster John Wilkinson had secretly bought out one of the two partners who leased the works to the Darbys and now he was tripling the waggonway rent to force them out of business. While the battle was bogged down in the courts (it took from 1757-1761 to sort it out) Abraham Darby II commissioned a pair of large engravings to advertise a positive image of the company, funded through 643 subscriptions, many paid by sympathetic Quakers. The moral is to never believe what you see in a work of art unless there is some corroborating evidence from archives, archaeological evidence and photographs.

Coalbrookdale came through this crisis and by 1800 the workforce had grown to one thousand. The catalyst had been the building of the Iron Bridge in 1779 under the direction of Abraham Darby III (1750-1789), pioneering another new use for cast iron, though this too caused major financial problems and once again artists were commissioned to show the Bridge and the valley in the best possible light. This was the first structural use of cast iron and the graceful 30 metre span caught the imagination of many artists and travellers. It can be seen as the first major advertising campaign, a bold statement about the versatility of the material. Its promoter commissioned William Williams (c1740-1798) to make an oil painting of the Bridge shown against the idyllic backdrop of the Gorge, which Darby then circulated through an engraving by the London scenery painter Michael Angelo Rooker (1743-1801) in 1781. Each purchaser also got a free copy of an engineering drawing. Thus purchasers could buy a picture of man's mastery over nature and they could not escape noticing that well-dressed sightseers were shown visiting the Iron Bridge on foot, in carriages and by boat, stopping to admire its beauty. There was little sign of the furnaces, forges or pollution.

To provide the 378½ tons of cast iron for the Iron Bridge while still meeting his business demands Darby had taken over Bedlam Furnace (pages 42/43) in 1776. Its location on the banks of the River Severn 450 metres downstream of the Bridge made it ideal, not only for bar iron

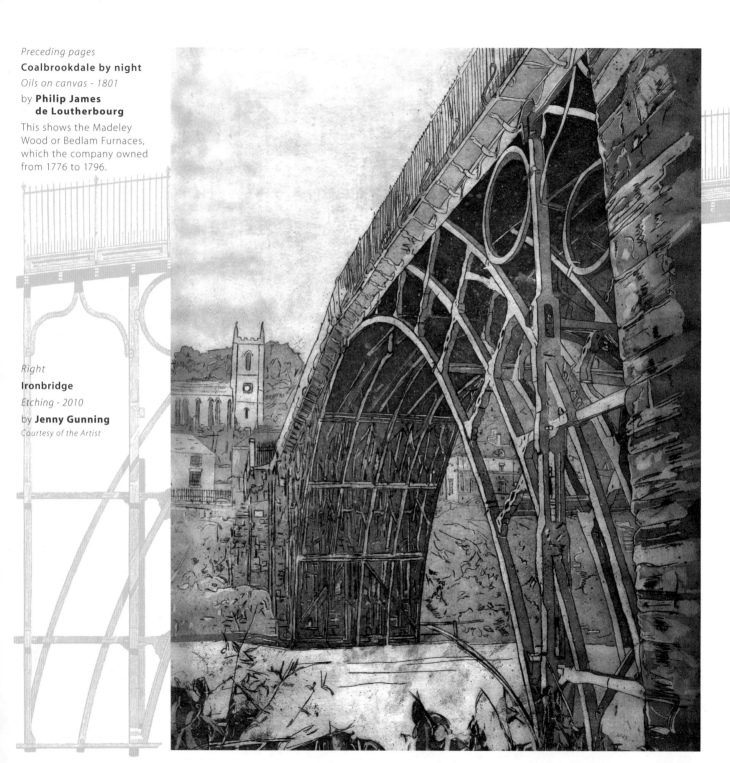

Preceding pages

Coalbrookdale by night

Oils on canvas - 1801

by **Philip James
de Loutherbourg**

This shows the Madeley
Wood or Bedlam Furnaces,
which the company owned
from 1776 to 1796.

Right

Ironbridge

Etching - 2010

by **Jenny Gunning**
Courtesy of the Artist

production, but also for re-melting the bars of pig iron into the large castings. Here they were loaded onto barges and the Iron Bridge was erected by lifting the castings directly from the boats. The worst flood on record occurred in February 1795 damaging or destroying virtually every bridge in Shropshire apart from the Iron Bridge. As a result three of the County's stone bridges were replaced in iron, cast by the Coalbrookdale Company, the first being the 40 metre span Buildwas Bridge by Thomas Telford in 1796. Two were built in Bath in 1800, two in Bristol in 1806, one in Jamaica in 1807 and the Wellington Bridge in Dublin. This was designed by John Windsor in 1815, a works foreman at Coalbrookdale and erected and opened in May 1816. A German traveller, Samuel H. Spiker, who had visited the Works noted that the cost 'was to be one thousand pounds sterling.' During this period the decisions about managing the Coalbrookdale Company were taken by the Partners who comprised of four women – Rebecca Darby (Abraham III's widow), Sarah Darby and Mary Rathbone (his sisters) and Deborah Darby, (his sister-in-law). A relatively unusual situation, but as Quakers each had received the same high standard of education as the men. The daily management was done by Quaker men however, initially Richard Dearman and then Barnard Dickinson.

As the easily-won minerals along the Severn were worked out, the seams were followed northwards in the Shropshire Coalfield, where they became deeper and required steam pumping and winding machinery to be profitable. The English topographical artist, Francis Nicholson (1753 -1844) recorded one of these new works (page 35) in 1820. The ironworks are believed to be Snedshill, about six kilometres from the market town of Shifnal and about six kilometres north of Coalbrookdale. The associated mines and two blast furnaces were owned by the great ironmaster John Wilkinson, but in 1807 they were absorbed into the giant Lilleshall Company. The dramatic effects of polluted skies had by this time become an accepted artistic approach and the scene is far from the polite views of the previous century. Gone are the romantic groups of labourers and picturesque landscapes. In their place are the plumes of black smoke from the mine engines and the acrid skies of heavy industry. Ironmaking did not stop in Coalbrookdale, but now the raw materials had to be

Left
Iron Bridge Porcelain Mug
This sublime porcelain mug with painted decoration evokes a peaceful view of what was a polluted and noisy region. Finished with gold lined borders it was aimed at weathier customers eager and proud to be associated with the new technology. It represents a more formal approach to the manufacture of souvenirs of the area.

brought in from further away using a network of canals begun in the 1780s. We get a glimpse of one of these works (page 34) recorded in 1847 by government inspector of mines Warrington Smythe. His small picture is informative but in no way an artistic interpretation because this man knew what he was looking at and simply recorded it. What is evident, however, is that the blast furnaces were getting bigger by this period and were being built in banks of three – again only possible if coke-fired.

Though the textile industry had organised itself to improve conditions in the first half of the 19th century, iron and steel workers did not establish any unions until the 1860s. Starting in the Black Country – the area on the northwest edge of Birmingham – several smaller societies amalgamated in 1887 and by 1891 had a nationwide union known as the Iron and Steel Trades Confederation. Their preoccupation was with working conditions, wages and medical support for their members, while the miners union had also been fighting to keep young children out of the mines. Despite various laws prohibiting children working under ground, the mine inspectors found frequent breaches of the regulations long after it became illegal.

To see more of this growth, we must look to another region of Britain – South Wales around Merthyr Tydfil. We can see something of the growth of Welsh ironmaking in the early years of the 19th century in a pen and wash sketch of 1817 by Thomas Hornor (1785-1844). It bears a close resemblance to an etching of the Penydarren Ironworks in J. G. Wood's book of 1813 *The Principal Rivers of Wales illustrated*, but Hornor's drawing shows the rolling mills at night with the shafts of light from the furnaces creating dramatic shadows against the smoke. Established in 1784 Penydarren was one of the three large ironworks close to Merthyr Tydfil. It was already the major iron

Ignite 9 tons of coke...

add 12 tons of preheated iron ore...

and 3 tons of limestone.

Heat until molten, just over 1600°c...

and pour into moulds... Allow to cool.

Making Iron - Cutaway diagram of an 18th century Blast Furnace

Coke is heated until it ignites, after which the other ingredients are added proportionately to keep the furnace fired and this is called 'the charge'.

An average 18th century furnace will then work continuously for around six months after which time it will be closed down and remedial works carried out.

Water powers two alternating bellows.

Limestone, iron ore and coke are mixed in proportionate measures prior to loading into the top of the blast furnace.

Pollution from iron production causes irreversible damage to human health, local food produce and the environment.

Molten iron when released from the furnace runs down channels on the 'pig bed' of sand.

This got its name as the smaller channels resemble piglets suckling from a sow.

Cams raise and lower the bellows to 'blast' air evenly through 'tuyeres' near the base of the furnace.

This raises the temperature to over 1600°c at which point molten iron is produced.

The impurities that form above the molten iron is called 'slag' and this is run off prior to the molten iron being released.

Images on these pages copyright and courtesy of the Ironbridge Gorge Museum Trust

A West View of the CAST IRON BRIDGE over the River Wear Sunderland Built by R Burdon Esq MP Begun Sep.r 24th 1793 Open'd Aug.t 9 1796 Span 236 feet Height 100 feet

Above

A west view of the cast iron bridge over the River Wear, Sunderland

The bridge was opened in 1796 with a span of 72 metres, then the longest in the world. This earthenware plaque was produced to commemorate the event and featured a canted scroll border and two holes for wall hanging.

producing area of South Wales in the 1780s before it expanded into coal. From 1802 on Merthyr Tydfil was linked by a tramroad worked by horses the 15 kilometres to the Glamorganshire Canal at Abercynon, which then went all the way down to the sea at Cardiff. This tramroad used cast iron rails for flangeless wheels to run on from 1791, the first ever appearance of all-iron rails. By 1840 Dowlais, one of the works near Merthyr, had fifteen furnaces producing an average of 1,370 tonnes of pig iron per week.

Another rival area that was eclipsing Coalbrook-dale was the northeast of England around Sunderland and Durham and rivers of the Tyne and Wear. Coal had been mined extensively since before 1700, most of it

shipped around the coast as far as London, some 480 kilometres further south. Iron ore was found in the same area, but it was the successful exploitation of railways that made the industrial growth of the region possible. Much of the early development was done by George Stephenson (1781-1848), whose first locomotive was built in 1814. One of the largest collieries was at Hetton about 13 kilometres southwest of Sunderland. The railway linking it to the ships on the River Wear was begun by George Stephenson in 1819 and opened in November 1822, the probable reason for the large lithograph by James Duffield Harding (1798-1863). It was claimed at the time to be the largest colliery in England. The whole line is shown in Harding's lithograph from the colliery on the far right to the River Wear on the far left, where we can see the great Sunderland Bridge of 1796, the largest cast iron bridge in the world at the time spanning 72 metres, over twice the size of the 1779 Coalbrookdale bridge. The railway was a mixture of gravity inclines, steep banks where the wagons were rope-hauled, and locomotive-hauled on the flat. After four kilometres hauled

A lavish, rural scene showing the Hetton Colliery in Co. Durham on the extreme right. On the extreme left with sailing vessels on the River Wear is Sunderland featuring one of the largest cast iron bridges of its day spanning the river.

**Coalbrookdale Company's
Top Works Foundry**

Photograph - 1901

Retired Coalbrookdale
foundry employees gather
in the foreground of this
remarkable photograph.
Younger employees at
the Top Works Foundry
assemble at the rear.

*Image opposite copyright and
courtesy of the Ironbridge
Gorge Museum Trust*

Richard Trevithick' Coalbrookdale Locomotive 1803

Richard Trevithick was an English inventor and engineer who pioneered
the design and use of high-pressure steam engines. To prove his theories
he built a stationary steam engine at Coalbrookdale in 1802. The machine
demonstrated enough promise that the Coalbrookdale Company embarked
on building the first rail locomotive to his design below in 1803.

Details are sketchy about the actual machine but a replica of this design
was built and still operates as a tourist attraction today.

Elevation drawing of Trevithick's Coalbrookdale locomotive 1803
Image on this page copyright and courtesy of the Science Museum, London

by a locomotive, the wagons were attached to a rope and hauled by stationary steam engines three kilometres up and over a hill, let down by rope for four kilometres, steam-hauled for another three kilometres, and finally run by gravity the last 780 metres to the '*staithes*' (cranes) on the river bank. Here the coal wagons were lifted out over barges by a crane and tipped into them. Rope-hauled railways remained common in many parts of the country until the 1830s, with even the major companies using them on parts of their lines. The Liverpool & Manchester of 1830 used a rope-hauled incline from Liverpool docks up to the main passenger station until 1896; the Canterbury & Whitstable Railway of 1830 only used locomotives for the last three kilometres of its nine kilometres route; and the London & Birmingham railway of 1836 rope-hauled its carriages and wagons up from Euston station one and a half kilometres to where it was flat enough to couple on locomotives.

The richness of the artists' images that began in Coalbrookdale and spread across the country is directly linked to the development of coke-smelting which had introduced new uses for iron in mining, transport, communications and machinery. As a result the English landscape changed from one of agriculture to industry, the effects of which captured the fertile imagination of topographical artists. Ever ready to embrace the current fashions, pictures often show that shift from idyllic views to more sinister depictions of hell on earth. So many of them were actually commissioned by companies and so the element of distortion is always a possibility. But the changes were far-reaching. Later paintings take the industrial development for granted and there is a growing fascination for the workers as the focus of the art.

Dublin Jack of All Trades

by Anonymous

I am a roving sporting blade, they call me Jack of all trades
I always found my chief delight in courting pretty fair maids
For when in Dublin I arrived to try for a situation
I always heard them say it was the pride of all the nation

In Baggot Street I drove a cab and there was well required
In Francis Street had lodging beds to entertain all strangers
For Dublin is of high renown, or I am much mistaken
In Kevin Street I do declare sold butter, eggs and bacon

On George's Quay I first began, I there became a porter
Me and my master soon fell out which cut my quaintance shorter
In Sackville Street a pastry cook, in James's Street a baker
In Cook Street I did coffins make, in Eustace Street a preacher

In Golden Lane I sold old shoes, in Meath Street was a grinder
In Barrack Street I lost my wife, and I'm glad I ne'er could find her
In Mary's Lane I've dyed old clothes of which I've often boasted
In that noted place Exchequer Street sold mutton ready roasted

In Temple Bar I dressed old hats, in Thomas Street a sawyer
In Pill Lane I sold the plate, in Green Street an honest lawyer
In Plunkett Street I sold cast clothes, in Bride's Alley a broker
In Charles Street I had a shop, sold shovel, tongs and poker

In Liffey Street* had furniture, with fleas and bugs I sold it
And at the bank, a big placard, I often stood to hold it
In New Street I sold hay and straw and in Spitalfields made bacon
In Fishamble Street was at the grand old trade of basketmaking

In Summerhill a coachmaker, in Denzille Street a gilder
In Cork Street was a tanner and in Brunswick Street a builder
In High Street I sold hosiery, in Patrick Street sold all blades
So if you wish to know my name, they call me Jack of all trades

Preceding pages
The Iron Bridge today in winter
Photograph - 2012
by **John Hallett**
Courtesy of the Artist

The Iron Bridge still stands today in its original position over the River Severn in the picturesque and aptly named town of Ironbridge, Shropshire.

Due to its excessive overall weight and the road traffic that used it a number of ribs have cracked. The bridge was closed to road traffic in 1934 but remains open to pedestrians.

Opposite
The view from Merchant's Arch during evening rush hour.
Photograph by the Author

* Liffey Street is adjacent to the bridge at the far right in this photograph

Distinctly
Pedestrian

The history of the Ha'penny Bridge

2

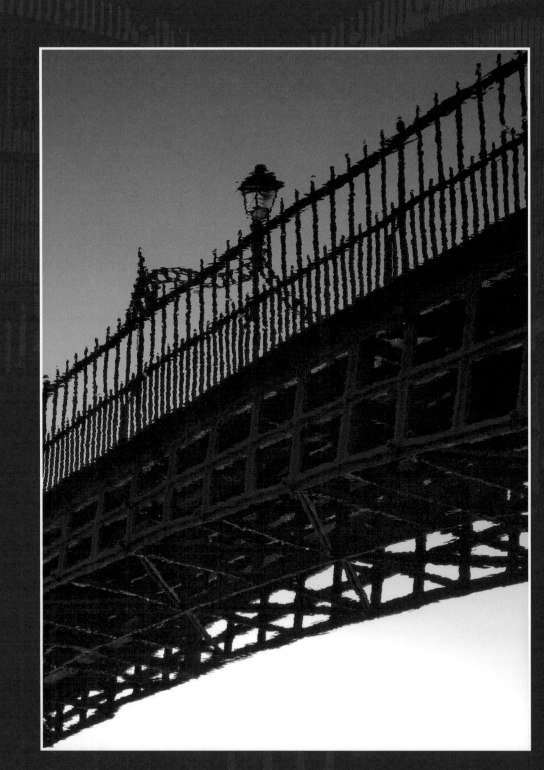

The history of the Ha'penny Bridge

by Gerard Smyth

The Liffey Bridges Project, 1987

In 1779 the first-ever iron bridge was constructed at Coalbrookdale in England. This bridge, though showing the use of iron, was but a solitary curiosity, as no other significant bridge was built in iron until the mid-1790s. Between 1795 and 1800 iron became a workable alternative for most bridges and following 1800 iron bridges became so common that they ceased to be curiosities. Optimism in the use of iron bridges was marked by Thomas Telford's

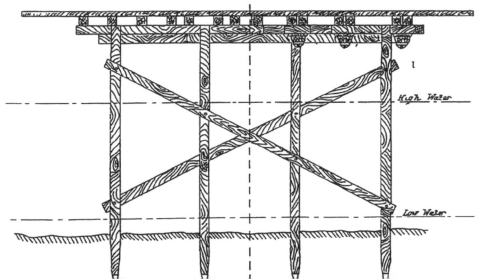

High Water

Low Water

Preceding pages

The Wellington Bridge after it first opened

Watercolour - 1818

by **Samuel F. Brocas**

A study of the bridge indicating it was originally painted black. This however was not the case as samples taken at the time of its restoration in 2001 indicated it was painted a creamy white colour. This was repeated for several decades before being painted in black and silver too.

Courtesy of Dublin City Council

Opposite

Network of iron

Photograph by the Author

Left

Bridge Crib or support

Because the bridge was cast in sections a temporary frame had to be built to support the emerging iron structure. Several 'cribs', made of wood like this one, had to be secured to the riverbed. Only after the bridge was fully constructed and tested were these wooden structures finally dismantled and removed.

Courtesy of Dublin City Council

proposal for London Bridge in 1801, which envisaged a massive single arch for 180 metres including 6,500 tons of iron. Soon after this, however, the whole approach to bridge building became more serious with several well-publicized collapses. Gradually the building of iron bridges spread to Ireland. The Wellington (or Ha'penny) footbridge of 1816 was probably the first iron bridge in Ireland, while the first road bridge was a short-span structure near Limerick erected in 1818.

Dublin in the 19th century was administered by an overmanned and elaborate public service, where many political and judicial posts were gained by breeding, influence or monetary status rather than by competence or capability. Thus the decision makers in Dublin were mainly

Below

Proposal for London Bridge by Thomas Telford - 1801

Lithograph
Size 30 x 72cm

Telford's bridge was regrettably never built due to the conservative nature of the developers who settled for a stone, arch bridge instead.

Could this design have influenced the design of the Ha'penny Bridge?

Protestants, scorned by the nationalists as *'shoneens'* and *'West Britons'* although they regarding themselves as an honourable part of the British connection. It is therefore no surprise to find that the Ha'penny Bridge was built privately under the instigation of two well-connected men, Alderman John Claudius Beresford and William Walsh, who had previously used their positions to lease the right to operate three Liffey ferries from Dublin Corporation – indeed Beresford was Lord Mayor of Dublin for the year 1814-15, the year the bridge was built. The bridge actually crosses the river near the site of one of these ferries, thereby replacing it. The embarkation point for the ferry on the north side was called Bagnio Slip which was approximately halfway between Carlisle

Opposite

The Ha'penny Bridge

Pencil Drawing
Size 30 x 72cm

by **Desmond McCarthy**

Courtesy of the Artist

Following page

The Wellington Bridge

Lithograph
Size 30 x 24cm

by **M Connor**

Lithographed by Holbrooke & Son

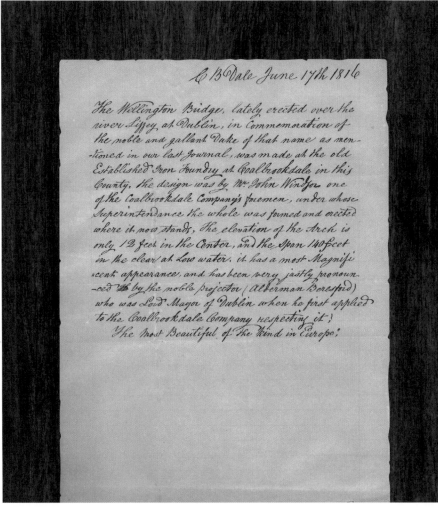

Above

**"The Most Beautiful
of the Kind in Europe"**

Written Journal

Notes written by John
Windsor, the bridge's
designer and foreman
of the Coalbrookdale
Works for the Salopian
Journal in 1816.

The bridge had just
been opened a month
earlier on 19 May.

(O'Connell) and Essex (Grattan) Bridges. Their motive in building the bridge was not one of philanthropy but was to line their own pockets with the takings charged for passage, as this bridge afforded a short cut to Crow Street Theatre, at that time the principal entertainment venue in the city.

Their motives may have been mercenary, but Beresford and Walsh constructed what was arguably Dublin's most elegant bridge. Its appearance has been amply described as 'a masterpiece of town-scape, lightly springing across the river in a delicate bow, its walkway spanned by graceful lamp bracket arches.' In 1815, Walsh applied to the Coalbrookdale Company for an estimate and received proposals from them for building a metal arch. These were approved by the Commissioners for Improving and Preserving the Port of Dublin and by Dublin Corporation providing that 'in the event of the Corporation finding that the erection of such a bridge be found objectionable or inconvenient, it shall within twelve months of their serving a notice taken down and removed, and the quay walls restored to a perfect state.' The developers also had to procure certificates as to the safety of the structure both from Francis Johnston, the well-known architect responsible for the General

Two views from the Ha'penny Bridge some 40 years apart.

During the 1970s and 80s huge swathes of Dublin were laid to waste as good, poor and dangerous buildings were demolished by developers eager to erect newer, higher density buildings. The top picture, taken in 1980 shows the destruction at Liffey Street and the effects of rebuilding with pastiche Georgian terraced apartments in the early 21st century.

Also of note are the different curvatures of the deck. In the top picture the deck meets the railing at each entrance at their mid point. This was revised when the bridge was renovated in 2001 with a long set of shallow steps making it easier for pedestrians to use.

Images on this pages courtesy of Dublin City Council

Post Office and from the architect John Semple, a relation of George Semple who rebuilt Essex Bridge in 1753 - 55. Permission was given, on condition that if the citizens of Dublin did not like it, the developers would have to take it down within six months.

The new iron bridge was opened on 19 May 1816 seemingly without any ceremony and for the first ten days all ten thousand pedestrians crossing were given free passage: after that they were charged a half penny, the same fee that had been charged for the former ferry at that location. At first the new bridge was unofficially named *Wellington Bridge* after the victor of Waterloo who was a native of Dublin – if famously an unwilling one! An English journal reported that: 'The Wellington Bridge lately erected over the river Liffey at Dublin in commemoration of the noble and glorious Duke of that name was made at the old established iron foundry at Coalbrookdale. The design was by John Windsor one of the Coalbrookdale foremen, under whose superintendence the whole was formed and erected where it stands. The elevation of the arch is only 3.6 metres in the centre and the span is 42 metres in the clear. At low water it has a magnificent appearance and has been pronounced by the noble projector (Alderman Beresford) "The most beautiful of the kind in Europe".'

The bridge itself is a single elliptical arch of cast iron consisting of three main ribs, each rib being cast in six separate lengths. The main structure was cast in eighteen sections for ease of transport during the long journey from Shropshire to Dublin. The pieces are thought to have been delivered first to the Greenpatch at Poolbeg by sailing ship. There they could be transferred by barges for transportation to their final destination. No records exist as to how the erection took place though we can speculate that some sort of temporary support – such as time cribs – was used. These piled cribs would have been placed at the joints in the ribs so that the bridge could be built out from the abutments or directly off barges making use of the tides. It is possible that no underpinning was used, rather a system of cables and heavy ropes supported the ribs or even lowered them though this is unlikely with the limitation of space which would have existed at the river side. The total cost of the bridge came to the round sum of three thousand pounds.

Below

The Half Penny Coin

This was the toll struck by the operators of the bridge when it first opened in 1816. It was coincidently the same as the fare charged by the ferries that operated at this point beforehand.

While Ireland used the British system of pounds, shillings and pence it issued its own currency with the name Hibernia (ancient Latin for Iverna or Ireland).

The name was located above the official representation of Hibernia, with harp and crown on the obverse side of a range of coins issued from 1660 onwards.

It has been calculated that In today's money (2016) the half penny would be worth € 0.57c approximately

Figures based on current inflation estimates.

It is quite interesting to look at the naming of this bridge. Although it was often referred to as *'Wellington Bridge'* in its early years, there is no record of it being officially named as such. The Duke of Wellington had been the hero of the Battle of Waterloo, fought in 1815. As Sir Arthur Wellesley he was chief secretary at Dublin Castle until 1808 having spent part of his childhood at Upper Merrion Street. In the bridge's early years it was sometimes caustically referred to as the *'Triangle Bridge'* – a sarcastic reference to John Claudius Beresford for his similarly named wooden scaffold used for flogging some of the 1798 rebels with a cat-o-nine-tails. This animosity was not helped when Beresford decorated Carlisle Bridge with the corpses of rebels. The public hatred was illustrated in 1798 when infuriated clients gathered outside Beresford's banking business and burned his promises to pay shouting 'What will he do now? His bank will surely break.'

Preceding pages

The bridge in 1953

The bridge pictured at high tide on a sunny spring morning. Compare this with the photograph on pages 176/7 and note how traffic ran in both directions on either quays before one-way systems had to be introduced.

In 1838, when the first Ordnance Survey maps of Dublin were published, it was titled *'Liffey Bridge'* and insofar as it has an official name, this is it. Down through the years, it has been referred to as the *'Metal Bridge'* and the Ha'penny Bridge, the name which is now popularly used.

In 1913 proposals were made for the replacement of the Ha'penny Bridge with an art gallery designed by the famous architect Sir Edwin Lutyens at the request of Sir Hugh Lane. The gallery would span the river similar to an example in Florence where the Uffizi Gallery runs over the river Arno. It was intended that the new Dublin gallery would be largely filled with pictures donated by Lane. However, there were objections to the proposal – some jealous people thought that Lane would be supplied with a monument at public expense. In the event, Dublin Corporation

Above

Advertising ignominy

The Bridge in a sorry state in the early 1900s with ugly advertising signage on three levels and also on the abutments on each side of the river.

Images on these pages courtesy of Dublin City Council

Opposite

Ha'penny Bridge
Watercolour - 2011
40 x 30cm
by **Kasper Zier**
Courtesy of the Artist

Above

Crossing the bridge

Pencil sketch

A drawing of the event attributed to the driver Dudley Colley.

Above right

Dudley Colley at the wheel of a sports car

Images courtesy of the Colley family

did not have enough funds for the project, so it was turned down. Annoyed with this, Lane determined to bequeath his paintings to the National Gallery in London and this was a bequest under his Will. However, Lane had a change of heart and before his untimely death on the Lusitania in 1915 he added a codicil to his Will leaving the paintings to Dublin. Unfortunately this was not witnessed and only after protracted negotiations was an agreement drawn up under which half the collection was held by the National Gallery and half by Dublin City Gallery the Hugh Lane with the collection being rotated every five years.

On 25 March 1919, after many years of complaints by Dublin citizens, the turnstiles were finally removed and the Metal Bridge declared toll-free to pedestrians. Prior to this, the bridge had passed into the hands of several individuals, until it finally reverted to Dublin Corporation after the 99 year lease had expired on 29 September 1916. On the freeing of the bridge the Irish Times reported that 'Dubliners have to discover the Metal Bridge' - the implication being that it saw little use by the general public while tolls were levied. The annual returns up to 1919, even after rent had been paid each year to the Corporation, had realised the cost of construction many times over. However, even though the tolls had gone, the toll-booths remained in place until a later date.

One of the more unusual stories regarding the bridge comes from Dudley Colley, who became a well-known racing driver of the 1930s. It seems that during a sojourn in a local hostelry with his university friends, he happened to remark that he had an ambition to cross the Metal Bridge

Right

Ha'penny Bridge, Dublin

Watercolour - 2012

23.5 x 17.5cm

by **John D Benson**

Courtesy of the Artist

in his 'baby' Austin. Colley takes up the story: 'I was not even consulted as to whether I was serious or not and a plan of campaign was worked out just as if I had not been present. Accordingly it was arranged that I should park my Austin in a narrow lane near the foot of the bridge, the others would patrol the quays on each side and occupy the attention of any stray policeman or officious citizen. At a given signal on a horn, I was to cross just like that. At my first attempt I misjudged the speed necessary to surmount the steps; the Austin stalled halfway up and I was forced to bump all the way down backwards. I made no mistake the second time, and was over and bouncing down the other side before anyone realised what was going on. I vanished up a side street and returned home by a devious route.' This is definitely the first and last time that the footbridge became a roadbridge and for any other aspiring University students it is not to be recommended. Another noted person associated with

Left

Ha'penny Bridge, Dublin

Lithograph - 2013
25 x 35cm
Edition of 75

by **Liam O'Broin**

Courtesy of the Artist

These two works show the bridge before and after its restoration in 2001.

The entrances on both sides of the river originally had cast iron railings (shown far left). These entrance areas were widened and the steps lowered during the bridge's restoration. The original railings were replaced with granite walls instead.

the Ha'penny Bridge was the late Hector Grey. The proprietor of a nearby shop selling all sorts of trinkets and toys, Grey was famous for his open-air bazzar, held on Sunday mornings at the northside of the bridge in Liffey Street.

It is a testimonial to the construction of the day that this elegant bridge has survived so long though there have been many false scares including a report in 1918 by the Borough Surveyor warning that 'if the worse condition of road and temperature should occur simultaneously, the bridge would fall.' In fact, the Ha'penny Bridge continued to retain the affections of Dubliners, and after the fall of Nelson's Pillar in 1966, it became an emblem of the city, a function which it retained until the Spire was completed in O'Connell Street in 2003. In 1971 the Corporation replaced the central decorative lamp bracket

arch which was in storage for several years and extensive repairs were carried out in 2001, which included bringing the bridge back to its original colour: for this work Dublin City Council received a European Union prize for Cultural Heritage at a ceremony in the Palais Egremont in Brussels in May 2003. Today, around 30,000 pedestrians cross the Ha'penny Bridge daily – the same number as O'Connell Bridge. The bridge is subtly lit by night which assists with pedestrian crossings and currently it is identified as the bridge where love locks are fixed. As the Ha'penny Bridge enters its third century in May 2016, it is secure in the affections of Dubliners and can enjoy an assured future.

Ill-mannered seagull

by Mártín Ó Direáin

Translated from the Irish
by Declan Collinge

Of all the men and women
In Dublin by the Liffey
Why, you scoundrel,
Did you bestow your gift on a poet?

Keep your filth to yourself
You voracious devious bird
And never besmear
This poet again while you live.

It's surely sad enough for me
That I steadily see
Your breed outstripping
The nobel seed of the swan.

Preceding pages

Eastern side of the Bridge in sunlight

The bridge is not a complete arc as might be first imagined. Rising gracefully from each abutment it flattens out in the centre to make it easier for pedestrians to traverse.

Also of note are the numerous cast iron sections that make up the arch.

Opposite

Gulls jostle

Photographs by the Author

The bridge
under threat

Hugh Lane's
vision for Dublin

3

Hugh Lane's vision for Dublin

by Logan Sisley

Exhibitions Curator, Dublin City Gallery The Hugh Lane

Preceding pages
Sir Edwin Lutyens' proposal for the Municipal Gallery of Modern Art over the River Liffey
Watercolour - 1913
by **William Walcot**
Courtesy of Dublin City Gallery The Hugh Lane

ne of the greatest threats to the Ha'penny Bridge during its lifetime was a 1913 plan to build an art gallery on its site. The gallery plan was advocated by Sir Hugh Lane who was attempting to find a permanent home for the art collection he and his supporters had given to the city of Dublin. The design for the Municipal Gallery of Modern Art by Sir Edwin Lutyens proved controversial and Dublin Corporation eventually voted against the proposal. The Ha'penny Bridge – or 'Metal Bridge' as it was then known – was therefore saved from destruction but the controversy over the future home of the gallery and Lane's conditional gift of priceless paintings would exercise the citizens of Dublin for many years to come.

The Municipal Gallery of Modern Art had opened in 1908 in temporary premises in Clonmell House, Harcourt Street. The gallery was the brainchild of Hugh Lane who had been motivated to do something for the visual arts in Ireland having seen an exhibition of John Butler Yeats and Nathaniel Hone, which was organised by Sarah Purser in 1901. Three years later Lane first exhibited the works that would form the nucleus of the collection for a Gallery of Modern Art along with other works on loan – notably from the Staats Forbes collection and the

Opposite
Sir Hugh Lane
Oil on canvas - 1913
by **Antonio Mancini**
Courtesy of Dublin City Gallery The Hugh Lane

Below
Another view of the proposed gallery
Pen and wash - 1913
by **William Walcot**

The proposed gallery viewed from Bachelor's Walk showing the immense size of just one of the two pavillions located on either side of the river.
Courtesy of Dublin City Gallery The Hugh Lane

impressionist dealer Paul Durand-Ruel – which Lane hoped would be purchased by others for the public collection. On 20 January 1908 the gallery opened with 300 works on display, all of which were presented by Lane himself and his supporters, including many artists. Lane also put on loan a group of continental paintings known as his conditional gift – including now celebrated works by Pierre-Auguste Renoir, Berthe Morisot, Édouard Manet and Claude Monet – which Lane said he would give to the city 'provided that the promised permanent building is erected on a suitable site within the next few years.'

Dublin Corporation voted £500 per annum towards running costs however the position of the gallery remained precarious in its first few years. Numerous schemes were advanced for a permanent home for a Gallery of Modern Art. As early as 1902 the architect Thomas Manly Deane proposed that the Royal Hibernian Academy and a Gallery of Modern Art be located on Clare Street so that all of the city cultural institutions were grouped together. Other suggestions included accommodating the collection within the National Gallery or the Metropolitan School of Art, or the provision of gallery space within the new Royal College of Science for Ireland (completed in 1911 and now the Government Buildings). Sites on Dawson Street, Kildare Street, Earlsfort Terrace, Lincoln Place and Merrion Square were also proposed; Lane objected to the latter as it was too far from the city centre and a gallery building would alter the symmetry of the square. As part of a wider city plan for a central highway with a new bridge running from Henry Street to Dame Street, another location was proposed in Temple Bar, where it might become 'a living protest against the mere materialism of commerce'. Proponents of this scheme objected to the bridge gallery at the Ha'penny or Metal Bridge site as it would have rendered their plans unworkable.

Opposite
Ha'penny Bridge, in shadow
Oil on canvas - 2002
61 x 76 cm
by **Brian Ballard**
Courtesy of the Artist

Lane engaged the architect Sir Edwin Lutyens, who had previously designed the garden at his London home, Lindsey House, and the Johannesburg Art Gallery, which Lane was instrumental in founding. Lutyens' first design for Lane took the form of a gallery pavilion in St. Stephen's Green, opposite the Royal College of Surgeons. Lutyens wrote to Lane on 12 October 1912 with an early sketch of the proposal, jesting that 'Faun nymphs or leprechauns could stand amongst the trees and Lord Ardilaun in front piazza.' A more fully realised plan was published in the Sunday Independent on 1 December 1912 following a meeting at the Mansion House at which it was resolved to collect public subscriptions for the new gallery. The St. Stephen's Green site was Lane's preferred option as he believed it would be both excellent for the gallery and do much 'for the popularising of the Green, which could be very much enjoyed as a resort for the citizens.' The proposal was not progressed due to the opposition of Lord Ardilaun who had bought the park and given it to the people of Dublin.

A barrier to the construction of a new gallery had been the Corporation's inability to raise the library rate to fund the venture. However in 1912 an act of Parliament was passed enabling the Corporation to levy the rate. On 21 January 1913 Dublin Corporation voted £22,000 towards the construction of a new gallery, based on ¼d in the £ on the library rate. The various arguments for and against were outlined at the meeting, arguments that would continue to exercise newspaper letter writers for months to come.

The motion in favour of the gallery was moved by the Lord Mayor Lorcan Sherlock and the deputation from the Citizens' Provisional Committee

of the Municipal Art Gallery was headed by Dermod O'Brien, President of the Royal Hibernian Academy. O'Brien noted the ongoing support of the Corporation for the gallery project since its founding and believed that the citizens would be proud if the paintings on loan were secured for the city. Other speakers stressed the educational and tourist value of the establishment of a permanent home for the gallery. The value of the works in jeopardy was debated, having been valued at £57,700 by Walter Armstrong, Director of the National Gallery of Ireland.

Objections were raised – notably that funds should not be diverted from desperately needed new housing or from the public libraries – but the motion was passed 33 votes to 4. William Martin Murphy, the powerful and wealthy newspaper, hotel and tramway proprietor, who was one of the sternest opponents of public funding for the gallery, was quick to show his disapproval. He congratulated 'the handful of dilettantes on their success in capturing such a handsome subsidy from such a democratic body like the Corporation for an object for which there is no popular demand, and one which will never be of the smallest use to the common people of this city.'

Days before the Corporation meeting W.B. Yeats, who was an important ally of Lane's in the establishment of the gallery, published the first of several poems associated with the gallery. It was published in *The Irish Times* on 11 January 1911 above a report on those who had recently offered subscriptions to the gallery fund. Published as *The Gift* and subtitled 'To a friend who promises a bigger subscription than his first to the Dublin Municipal Gallery if the amount collected proves that there is considerable 'popular demand' for the pictures',

Above

Homage to Sir Hugh Lane

Oil on Canvas - 1920

by **Sean Keating**

Gathered around John Singer Sargent's 1906 portrait of Hugh Lane are several of Lane's most ardent supporters: Thomas Bodkin, Dermod O'Brien, Thomas Kelly, W B Yeats, George Russell (AE), Col. Hutchinson Poe and Richard Caulfield Orpen. Behind the group is a view of Lutyens' Bridge Gallery seen from O'Connell Bridge against a rich red sunset.

Courtesy of Dublin City Gallery The Hugh Lane

91

Right

Ha'penny Bridge

Etching - 2013
34 x 24 cm
Edition of 50

by **Sarah Rogers**

Courtesy of the Artist

the poem unfavourably compared Dubliners who were reticent to give to Lane's project to artistic patrons of Renaissance Italy:

Leave Paudeens to their pitch and toss,
Look up in the sun's eye, and give
What the exultant heart calls good
That some new day may breed the best
Because you gave, not what they would,
But the right twigs for an eagle's nest

Having secured the support of Dublin Corporation, Lane's supporters worked to collect subscriptions for construction costs over the agreed £22,000 and to secure a suitable site. The Abbey Theatre contributed to fund-raising efforts selling handkerchiefs featuring drawings by John Butler Yeats on their tour of the United States of America in 1913. They also gave benefit performances on their return to Dublin in May that year.

Above

Promoting the cause overseas

A linen handkerchief featuring leading Irish playwrights and actors, eliciting support for the gallery that was sold on the Abbey Players tour of the United States in 1913.

Following the rejection of the Stephen's Green plan, Lane considered a bridge site the second best option. An extension to Carlisle (now O'Connell) Bridge was first proposed – but Lane thought the bridge 'such a perfect thing in itself and in relation to Sackville Street that it should not be altered' – then Grattan Bridge was considered. The idea was quick to draw opposition, not least as it would block the view westwards of the setting sun, but the proposal had the benefit that it did not require the purchase of land.

In January 1913 the Waterford engineer, William Friel, was approached by Francis Brownrigg Craig of the Office of Public Works on behalf of the Mansion House Committee for advice on the cost of foundations for a bridge gallery. Craig believed Friel could benefit from the scheme 'if the thing is not from the outset financially damned'. He wrote that the Committee wouldn't hear of it being sited at Carlisle Bridge and wanted it put at Grattan Bridge. Friel initially provided costs for reinforced

Following page

Sketch of the proposed gallery viewed from O'Connell Bridge

Pen and Ink - 1913

by **William Walcot**

Courtesy of Dublin City Gallery The Hugh Lane

concrete foundations at Grattan Bridge which he reckoned at £10,751.18s.

The Irish Times argued that it could 'hardly be said to have an artistic environment' and that the 'adjacent buildings were of a 'prosy character'. It said the utilitarian surroundings would pose a challenge to any architect 'who would make his building ornamental, without having the air of being dumped down in hopelessly inappropriate surroundings.' William Corrigan objected to the plan on the basis that 'cheapness and nearness should not outweigh other and weightier considerations' and that the obstruction of the views east and west along the Liffey would 'shut out as real beauty as it would contain, and be a still greater sin against art and nature'. This objection featured prominently when the plan was shifted eastwards to the Metal Bridge site, which Lane preferred to the Grattan Bridge proposal. The latter met his criteria as outlined in *The Irish Times*: 'I want the building to justify its existence, not merely as a house for the pictures, but as a place of resort for the citizens. I want it to be beautiful in an advantageous position, and as I want it to become familiar and well-used, it is essential that its position should be close to the principal centre of traffic.'

In 1913 the Metal Bridge was still under a lease to a toll operator – hence the name the Ha'penny Bridge – but would revert to Dublin Corporation in 1916, at which point the site would become available for the gallery. The toll bridge was then covered with advertising and was widely regarded as an eyesore. Its demolition was therefore one of the arguments in favour of the scheme on that site. Lane proposed that construction of the new bridge could begin in advance of the expiry of the lease and the

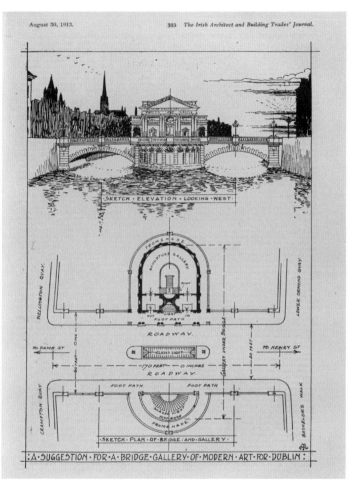

Above

An alternative plan for a bridge gallery by Horace T. O'Rourke

This design lined the gallery on an East - West axis in the middle of the Liffey. This would have considerably reduced the overall bulk of the Lutyens proposal but was only half the size of the one being objected to by Dubliners and others.

Reproduced courtesy of the Board of Trinity College Dublin

demolition of the Metal Bridge as it would not necessarily be on the same line as the existing bridge. In March 1913 William Friel provided costs based on driving piles clear of the existing abutment walls, which totalled £10,644.11s.

Lane engaged Edwin Lutyens to work on plans for the bridge gallery although he was never officially commissioned by Dublin Corporation. The architect's scheme consisted of two neoclassical pavilions at either side connected by a foot bridge with a colonnade allowing for views through the structure, which may have been intended to counter arguments that the building would have blocked views of the setting sun. William Walcot produced detailed perspective drawings of the proposed building, showing the gallery integrated into the life of the city. On one, a Guinness barge passes underneath indicating that it would not interfere with commerce on the river. A view to the east shows the dome of the Custom House in the distance and that to the west shows Christ Church Cathedral. In contrast the *Irish Independent* published an alternative uncredited scheme that emphasised the bulk of the building and 'how much out of harmony it would be with its surroundings'.

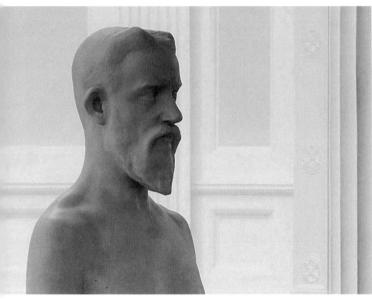

Like Lane, W. B. Yeats favoured the bridge site as it provided 'an opportunity for a building that will become – partly from the strangeness of its position, partly I believe, from its beauty – one of the most famous characteristics of the town.' He felt it would add to the scene from Carlisle (O'Connell) Bridge providing a 'touch of ornament, of conscious pleasure and affection.' The same day William Martin Murphy bemoaned the fact that 'one would think that Sir Hugh Lane owned Dublin, and that he could command the Corporation to erect a building in his honour on any public site that he decreed'. He argued that Lane wanted to disfigure the city with the bridge gallery and cautioned that the value of the paintings was questionable given the changes in fashion in the art world: 'What their value will be in twenty or thirty years' time, when, perhaps, the 'Futurists' or the 'Cubists' come to their own, no one can tell.' He reserved special criticism for Labour members of the Corporation, arguing that it wouldn't create significant employment but the 'shrine of modern French art'

Left

Ha'penny for your thoughts

Linocut - 2013
20 x 30.2cm
Edition of 20

by **Mary Grey**

Courtesy of the Artist

would be decorated with largely imported materials. In contrast, the Labour movement leader Jim Larkin backed the Gallery project, and declared that William Martin Murphy, for his meanness in the matter of Sir Hugh Lane's offer, would be condemned to keep an art gallery in Hell.

Despite the growing controversy surrounding the project, on 19 March 1913 Dublin Corporation voted 28 to 5 in favour of the bridge gallery. Yet the debate did not end there. On a visit to Dublin the writer George Bernard Shaw gave a tongue-in-cheek interview to *The Irish Times*, enquiring 'has Sir Hugh

Lane ever smelt the Liffey?' Shaw was in fact a supporter of the gallery, having donated a bust of himself by Auguste Rodin in 1908. When asked if he thought Lane's collection valuable he responded: 'Think it! It is valuable. Is anybody in Dublin so stupendously ignorant as not to know that it will be one of the most precious collections of the kind in Europe?' Shaw, however, favoured locating the gallery in Merrion Square to make that area of the city a cultural Acropolis. He said a visit would be more interesting than going to the South Pole, because 'several people have been to the South Pole, and nobody has ever been inside Merrion Square since the six days of creation.' When asked if the Square would be too far from the city's poor he lambasted: 'Our object is to preserve good pictures for ever and to get rid of the poor at the earliest opportunity... The poor will burn your pictures some day if you do not make an end of poverty.'

Below

The War Memorial Gardens, Islandbridge

Sir Edwin Lutyens also designed these commemorative gardens to honour Irish soldiers who had died during the First World War.

Note the similarities in the design and style of both buildings.

Photograph by the Author

George Moore, on the other hand, called Shaw a sentimentalist, and was filled with horror at the thought of Merrion Square's 'quiet gentilities invaded by endless streams of gaping visitors.' He dismissed any educational value the gallery might have and hoped Lane might introduce a small orchestra, as 'good pictures bore rich and poor alike.' He backed the bridge plan and when the question of it obstructing the view was raised he remarked: 'You mean the very foolish sunset that is always going on over Chapelizod, in that direction? If Lane succeeds in abolishing that sunset he will have done a great deal for Dublin'.

While plans were progressing and funds were forthcoming it was clear that the bridge gallery would still face numerous obstacles in finding a new home. The objections were numerous, ranging from the practical –

Following pages

Aston Quay

Oil on canvas - 2007
40 x 50 cm

by **Francis Matthews**

Courtesy of the Artist

that a river site would be prone to flooding – to the social – that the working people of Dublin were not interested in paying for art. The recurring argument that it would block the view up the Liffey was addressed by the *Saturday Herald's* cartoonist Gordon Brewster who proposed that the gallery should be erected on the top of Nelson's Pillar 'where it could not obstruct any view of the city.' The Town Planning and Housing Association objected on the basis that it would render obsolete its proposal for a new north-south central street. William Martin Murphy and others argued that the building was a waste of money that would be better spent on housing.

The issue was repeatedly debated at Dublin Corporation meetings. On 23 June a report by Edwin Lutyens was read out at a special meeting of the Corporation. The architect argued that Lane's preferred location presented a fine opportunity from an architectural point of view in that it would be seen from Carlisle Bridge and that it would restore vitality to the heart of the city. It would also 'do away with the present ugly Metal Bridge and its blatant advertisements, which cannot under any circumstances be said to add to the beauty of the city.' The cost of construction was put at £43,000; there being a shortfall of £10,000 given the £22,000 promised by Dublin Corporation and the £11,000 then raised by subscriptions. Lutyens said he would favour a home for the collection at the Mansion House should a bridge gallery prove impossible. The motion to adopt the Mansion House Committee's recommendations of the Metal Bridge site was defeated and the matter was deferred to a sitting of the whole house. At another meeting of 21 July, Sarah Cecilia Harrison reported that Lane had written to her expressing his impatience

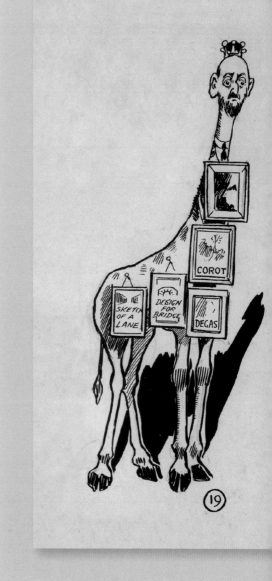

ART GALLERY ④

and if the matter was not settled within a few days the pictures would be lost to Dublin. Harrison was a painter and key ally of Lane and had compiled the first catalogue of the Municipal Gallery of Modern Art in 1908. She was also the first woman to be elected to Dublin Corporation in 1912.

In early August Lane returned to Dublin and removed the loan paintings from the Harcourt Street Gallery to the Mansion House. He met with a committee from the Corporation and explained that the paintings would go on loan to a London gallery until the Dublin building was complete. He would sign over the paintings to Dublin Corporation once its member had agreed to proceed with the Bridge site and he vowed to cover any construction costs in excess of £45,000.

Lane's intervention might have galvanised support for the retention of the paintings in Dublin but the political context had become increasingly difficult during a period of social and economic tension. The Strike and Lock-out began in August 1913 and lasted through the winter to January 1914, causing extreme hardship and polarised the population. The business community was led in the dispute by Lane's arch-rival, William Martin Murphy. In September 1913 tenement houses in Church Street collapsed killing seven people, heightening tension and highlighting the urgency of the city's housing problem. Dublin had dramatically changed from 1904 when Lane first exhibited the pictures that would form the nucleus of the modern art gallery. These diverse yet interconnected issues were satirised by Frank Reynolds who depicted the various factions as animals in the Dublin Zoo. Alongside politicians, labour and women's suffrage activists, ratepayers and

slum landlords, Lane was shown as a giraffe with pictures hanging from his neck – including *'Design for Bridge'*; William Martin Murphy was shown as a dog with the gallery as his bone.

Furthermore there was the ongoing debate over Ireland's relationship to the United Kingdom and the nationality of the architect for the Gallery of Modern Art became contentious. Even before Lutyens' plans were publicly revealed *The Irish Architect* expressed the hope that: 'architects and others interested in the encouragement of native effort will refrain from giving any financial support to this project until the Committee publicly declare that it is not their intention to boycott the architectural profession in Ireland.' Horace O'Rourke (who as City Architect would later design the gallery's eventual home on Parnell Square) published his own proposal for a bridge gallery in *The Irish Architect*, of which he was editor. Although Luytens' mother was Irish by birth, this was insufficient to quell the critics. Lane stressed that regardless of the choice of architect, 'all the money subscribed... will be spent in Ireland, and when the scheme comes to be carried out it should mean a good deal of work for Dublin labour.' When the matter was again addressed at a

special meeting of Dublin Corporation on 8 September 1913, W. T. Cosgrave put forward a motion that no proposal for the erection of a Municipal Art Gallery could be contemplated which excluded Irish architects from the design competition. The vote was not carried but the bridge gallery project finally hit an insurmountable hurdle at the same meeting. Sarah Cecilia Harrison moved that should the Mansion House Committee raise the necessary funds to meet the shortfall up to £45,000 the Council agree to Lane's wishes without delay. The vote was lost 23 to 21.

On the day the councillors met, W. B. Yeats published in *The Irish Times* another poem venting his frustration at the lack of support for Lane's venture. It was printed as *Romance in Ireland* (On reading much of the

Right

**A painting
from a painting**

Oil on Canvas - 1920

by **Sean Keating**

Sean Keating's painting of the proposed gallery over the Liffey as seen from O'Connell Bridge from his picture *'Homage to Sir Hugh Lane'* reproduced on page 91.

This clearly shows the gallery dominating the view to the west at sunset. The blocking of the sunset by the proposed gallery became just one of the reasons why the gallery was objected to in this location.

Courtesy of Dublin City Gallery The Hugh Lane

correspondence against the Art Gallery) but later became known as *September 1913* and begins:

What need you, being come to sense,
But fumble in a greasy till
And add the ha'pence to the pence,
And prayer to shivering prayer, until
You have dried the marrow from the bone,
For men were born to pray and save?
Romantic Ireland's dead and gone -
It's with O'Leary in the grave.

Hugh Lane, as he had indicated, shipped the disputed works to London where they were placed on loan to the National Gallery. He also bequeathed them to the London institution but remained optimistic that the Dublin gallery issue would be resolved. On a visit to America in 1914 Lane expressed the hope that the coming of Home Rule would see a resolution of the conflict over the bridge. It was reported that 'he has been agitating to secure a permanent building and hopes that when Home Rule comes he will get one. He thinks municipalities rather slow to appreciate the educational value of fine paintings.' In 1914 Lane was appointed Director of the National Gallery of Ireland. In another generous act he donated his salary of £500 to a purchase fund for pictures and also presented a group of old masters to the National Gallery of Ireland.

In mid-April 1915 Lane travelled to New York. On his return voyage the ship on which he was travelling, the Lusitania, was sunk by a German submarine on 7 May off the Cork coast, not far from his birthplace. His body was never recovered. However a signed codicil to his will in which he bequeathed the continental pictures to Dublin was found after his death. As the codicil was not witnessed it was deemed invalid and a lengthy battle ensued over the legitimate ownership of the paintings. A 1926 British parliamentary enquiry determined that they belonged to London although this did not put an end to the campaign to return them to Dublin, by then the capital of the Irish Free State.

Five years after Lane's death, his achievements – and the controversy over the gallery building – were remembered in a painting by Seán Keating. Homage to Sir Hugh Lane, 1920, was commissioned by Lane's friend, Dr Thomas Bodkin, who was later Director of the National Gallery of Ireland. Bodkin was commissioned by the Irish government

SATURDAY HERALD, APRIL 12, 1913.

ART GALLERY SITE IN DUBLIN ---ANOTHER SUGGESTION.

MUNICIPAL ART GALLERY

In view of the recent controversy regarding the site for a Municipal Art Gallery, our artist ventures to suggest the top of Nelson's Pillar, where it could not obstruct any view of the city.

Above

Art Gallery Site in Dublin - Another Suggestion

Illustration - 1913

by **Gordon Brewster**

The *Saturday Herald's* satirist takes a swipe at the shenanigans going on.

Courtesy of Dublin City Gallery The Hugh Lane

in 1932 to write Hugh Lane and his Pictures in which he argued for the return to Dublin of the 39 modern pictures in Hugh Lane's Bequest to the National Gallery, London. Gathered around John Singer Sargent's 1906 portrait of Hugh Lane are several of Lane's most ardent supporters: Thomas Bodkin, Dermod O'Brien, Thomas Kelly, W. B. Yeats, George Russell (AE), Colonel Hutchinson Poe and Richard Caulfield Orpen. Behind the group is a view of Lutyens' Bridge Gallery seen from O'Connell Bridge against a rich red sunset.

Keating's painting now hangs in Dublin City Gallery The Hugh Lane – as the gallery Lane founded is now called – in Parnell Square. It opened on its present site, Charlemont House, in 1933, thanks to the concerted efforts of many people including the painter Sarah Purser. She is absent in the painting but is obliquely represented by the table covering, which had belonged to her. Absence and loss – of a building and of a collection of paintings – is a recurring theme in this story. When the gallery first opened in Charlemont House in 1933 a room was left empty – except for a bust of Lane by Albert Power – awaiting the return of the disputed paintings. And return they have; since 1959 a series of agreements have enabled the works to be shared between the two institutions. In 2008 all 39 paintings from the Lane Bequest at the National Gallery, London, were shown for the first time together in his Dublin gallery's permanent home. The exhibition, *Hugh Lane: 100 Years*, marked the centenary of the founding of the institution. It also included William Walcot's images of Lutyens' plans for the Ha'penny Bridge site, three of which Lane bequeathed to Dublin's Municipal Gallery of Modern Art and which bear witness to the tumultuous events in the story of the gallery and of the Ha'penny Bridge.

Liffey Bridge

by Oliver St. John Gogarty

I gazed along the waters in the West,
Watching the low sky colour into flame,
Until each narrowing steeple I could name
Grew dark and the far vapours, and my breast
With silence like a sorrow was possessed,
And men as moving shadows went and came;
The smoke that stained the sunset seemed like shame,
Or lust, or some great evil unexpressed.

Then with a longing for the taintless air,
I called that desolation back again,
Which reigned when Liffey's widening banks were bare:
Before Ben Edair gazed upon the Dane,
Before the Hurdle Ford, and long before
Fionn drowned the young men by its meadowy shore.

Preceding pages
Surface disturbance
Photograph by the Author

Opposite
The Liffey Boardwalk

The Liffey Boardwalk was an initiative of Dublin City Council to provide more space along the river for pedestrians hemmend in by heavy traffic on both quays.

It was built in stages along the city's north quays facing south and connects most of the city centre bridges. It has become an unqualified success especially in warmer months when thousands of Dubliner's and visitors alike gather to absorbe the city's ambiance, free of the nearby traffic.

Photograph by the Author

The pint *of* plain

Shipping the
black stuff overseas

4

Shipping the
black stuff overseas

by Michael English

Black Mountain Design Company

Preceding pages

A Guinness barge heads back to the brewery

The Guinness barge *Killiney* approaches the Ha'penny Bridge during the early 1960s laden with empty barrels as it heads back upriver.

Courtesy of Guinness Archives

Below

Early advertising

A painted wooden sign proudly showing two views of the brewery, the river and barges.

On the very last day of the year 1759 and at the age of just 34, Arthur Guinness signed one of the longest leases (page 121) ever recorded in Dublin's history. This lease covered an existing brewery and adjacent land at St. James's Gate on the city's western outskirts. It was a bold and confident gesture of a man who had brewing in his blood since he was a young man. Somehow he knew to his core that his destiny would be to found one of the world's great brewing companies and one that still bears his name. That it would be based in one of the world's smaller countries and surrounded by water wasn't going to put Guinness off either. While distribution of his product presented a major problem for the young brewer, it would also present a challenge. Over the next one hundred and fifty years it would become one of the most efficient beer transportation systems in the world.

What Guinness couldn't have foreseen however was that his product would become the country's preferred and most recognized tipple.

Opposite page

Arthur Guinness

A portrait of Arthur Guinness, the founder of the brewery.

Images on these pages courtesy of Guinness Archives

Not only that but over time it would also inveigle its way into the country's very fabric and become a major part of its culture too. As the brewery expanded, so did its dominance and influence to the point where it became one of the city's major industries and icons. Another structure, that eventually found iconic status was the Ha'penny Bridge, which lay further downstream, east of St. James's Gate. While both were utterly different in their design and purpose both the brewery and bridge in their own ways, have contributed to the city's changing fortunes ever since.

Although his Protestant family could trace their lineage back to the Gaelic clans of Co. Down, Arthur Guinness himself was born in Celbridge in Co. Kildare in 1725 and and grew up as part of a well-to-do Anglo-Irish family. His father Richard Guinness was a land steward and managed a nearby estate for Dr. Arthur Price, who later became the protestant Archbishop of Cashel.

Apart from looking after his flock one of Price's other interests was brewing and he assumed control of the Kildrought Brewery at Leixlip on the River Liffey, some 13 kilometres west of Dublin in 1722. As part of Richard's stewardship of the estate he would have also been expected to oversee the operation of this brewing concern too. Richard Guinness and the Archbishop obviously had a good relationship, as Price became the boy's godfather, which might have prompted him to being named Arthur too. No doubt some of his father's interests including brewing rubbed off on the young man as in 1755 Arthur Guinness along with his brother took over the lease on a brewery in Leixlip, partially funded by a generous inheritance from the Archbishop.

It was however, in his role as Archbishop of Cashel that Arthur Price elevated himself to a level of notoriety that he could never imagine. Soon after being appointed to the post in 1744 he vetoed plans, already in place to repair and

restore the old cathedral on the Rock of Cashel, one of the principal jewels of Irish medieval architecture. After first gutting the interior and then removing the roofs of the complex he proceeded to build the Cathedral of St. John on the far side of Cashel in 1783. The greatest irony of this willful act of vandalism is that thousands now visit the ruins on the rock every day compared with the trickle of visitors who make it to St. John's.

Arthur Guinness by this time had gained significant experience and business acumen in the art of brewing, site management, storage and

Above

The Brewery Lease

A copy of the original lease is now embedded in a glass case in the floor of the Guinness Storehouse in Dublin.

Images on these pages courtesy of Guinness Archives

distribution. With a clearer, bolder vision of what could be achieved on an even greater scale in the years to come, he handed over the Leixlip brewery to his brother to run and struck out for the capital in 1759.

St. James's got its name from the local holy well in the vicinity on the city's western side. St. James's Gate was a large structure that straddled the road here and marked one of the original entrances to the city of Dublin during the Middle Ages. This gate was tolled and people needing to enter the city here paid for the privilege of doing just that.

The land around St. James's had previously been controlled by the Rainsford family for many years and who also ran a prosperous brewing concern marketing their brew simply as Rainsford's Beer. Sir Mark Rainsford, a city alderman and Lord Mayor (1700-01) had been passed on water rights from his father-in-law Giles Mee that he then leveraged to establish a new brewery and is generally credited with founding the brewery at St. James's Gate. When Sir Mark died in 1709 the family's interest in brewing fell into decline over the years that followed. This was due in part to the strong competition from other brewers and the almost identical brews they produced. The brewery was leased out to a Captain Espinasse who ran it successfully until his untimely death in 1750, falling from his horse after a visit to an inn in Drogheda. For nearly ten years the brewery lease garnered little attention until it passed into the hands of the second Mark Rainsford who managed to interest Arthur Guinness in the premises. In 1759 a very confidant Guinness signed the lease for a period of nine thousand years for the land at an annual rent of some £45.

At this time the people of Ireland and Britain were no strangers to a variety of beers available and produced locally. Porter was a dense, dark drink probably derived from other strong brown ales and was first known

PORTER.

of in the early 18th century as being popular with London's river and street porters - hence the name. This developed alongside another style of stronger, darker beer called stout, more in reference to its strength although this changed over time to mean body and colour too.

In taking on the lease Guinness decided to produce something a little less ordinary from that of the other breweries and settled on this relatively new style of beer - stout. Guinness itself is a dark dry stout derived from roasted unmalted barley, hops and yeast, and while it might look black it is actually a dark, ruby red in colour. Unlike other dark malts Guinness is made from unmalted barley grain that is roasted at high temperature while being lightly sprayed with water to prevent it from burning. This particular technique produces the beer's iconic dark colour. Nitrogen introduced in the 1960s is now used in the unique ritual of pulling the pint, which takes place in two distinct phases and gives Guinness its creamy head. When first presented with a pint or glass you'll notice an aroma, which is sweet smelling with a malty, coffee nose. On tasting the brew you'll notice a wonderful fusion of roasted and bitter flavours combining on a smooth creamy balanced palate.

Guinness had carefully chosen the St. James's site as the area had been associated with brewing from the 17th century onwards. This was to service the growing local market and compete with the burgeoning London brewers who viewed Dublin with its growing population and status as a lucrative prize. More importantly it was an area where a brewery could access generous supplies of clean water that were prevalent in the surrounding wells. The water

13/50   Hapenny Bridge in mirror   Daniel Lipstein

Left

**Ha'Penny Bridge,
View from the Grand
Social, Spring 13**

*Etching and
Dry Point - 2013
38 x 29cm
Edition of 50*

by **Daniel Lipstein**

Courtesy of the Artist

Following pages

**The Guinness barge
Castleknock unloads
casks of beer**

A busy day in Dublin
Port with three Guinness
ships at the quay walls
adjacent to Gandon's
Custom House.

Guinness House Flag

This red pennant with
a black letter '*G*' was flown
on all the Guinness ships
and is referred to as the
company's '*House Flag*'.

*Images courtesy of
Guinness Archives*

quality in Dublin was generally declining as the population increased. The growing amount of effluent that was discharged daily into the Liffey and the other rivers for disposal also contaminated the fresh water. Beer and ale were actually more commonly consumed than water, as it was perceived to be free of the contaminants in water that were removed during the brewing process.

The original four acre site with its frontage on James's Street is complemented with the iconic gate that still stands to this day and marks the original entrance. To the rear, the site extended to Portland Street with further entrances for the delivery of raw goods needed for brewing and the departure of the finished product. The buildings on the site at the time comprised of a copper, a kieve, a mill, two malthouses, stabling for twelve horses and a loft to hold 200 tons of hay. These horses were an important side of the business as once the stout had been produced it had to be distributed and done so by the brewery in an orderly fashion. Allowing individual publicans to pick-up and drop off beer barrels at what ever time suited them would have led to total chaos in the yards and surrounding streets as other breweries operated in the area as well.

Guinness used horses extensively throughout the brewery and in the delivery of beer to Dublin's ale houses. Clydesdales and Percheron horses were the preferred breeds as these were large, strong animals that had real pulling power. Every horse at the brewery was individually named and these included *William, Roy, Cecil* and *Bruce* for example. The horses were sometimes used in pairs depending on the weight of the loads they hauled and these sets had paired names such as *Pride & Prejudice, Thunder & Lightening* and *Rhyme & Reason*. From the beginning Guinness had its own team of horses and these were stabled within the brewery highlighting the importance of the horse in brewery life.

Many of the horses performed special duties within the brewery itself, hauling casks, heavy machinery, bulk liquids and raw ingredients while others were attached to the various carts, trailers and wagons in use outside the brewery. Special instructions had to be drawn up to manage the team, which could run into thousands at peak times. All the horses received the highest quality of stabling, care and nutrition. Each horse had three meals a day, some of whom would even be on special diets.

With the opening of the two main canals in the late 18th century Guinness became aware of the huge carrying capacity of these newly introduced vessels called barges. This enabled the brewery to ship larger quantities of the beer to people outside Dublin for the first time. The canals made their way to the west and south and even more horses were employed to pull the barges as they travelled as far as the Shannon as well as up and down it. This had a positive knock-on effect as it became easier for

Below

Loading the floats

Guinness horses were well shod and looked after. Here some of them are assembled outside one of the beer filling sheds with wooden casks on a variety of floats.

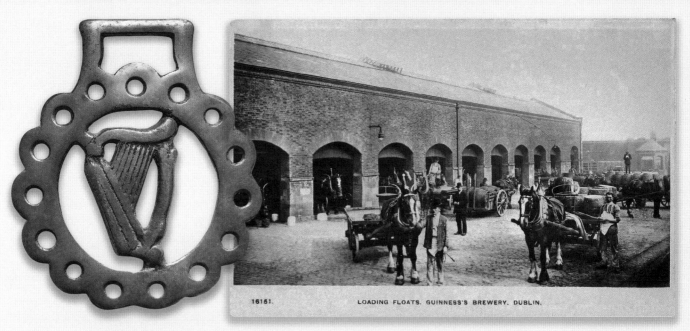

16151.   LOADING FLOATS. GUINNESS'S BREWERY, DUBLIN.

Guinness for the first time to bring in the raw materials for beer production such as the barley in bulk for the ever expanding brewery. Because of its size and importance Guinness even had a spur off the Grand Canal with its own dock within the brewery itself.

While the horse had provided the ability to move huge loads within the brewery, on the canals and on the roads its days were numbered after the ending of the Second World War in 1945. Great strides had been made in terms of transport technology, first on the railways and then on the roads, which was now much faster, and outpacing the leisurely pace of the canals. Petrol and diesel were now also available in increasing measures after a glut throughout the war years. Guinness saw the changes coming and reacted accordingly, employing in ever greater numbers,

Above left

A horse's brass

Each horse had one of these special brass insignia plates.

These were mounted on the bridle to identify it with Guinness since the brewery had registered the harp as their official symbol in 1876.

Images on these pages courtesy of Guinness Archives

131

Lionn Oub Oúbalza Ṡuinness
sinne do oḃḃunt agus do ċur amaċ
mar marc cráoála agus vuilleóg againn
an n-a ċur i mbuiⱃéil ag
ná cuireann i mbuiⱃéil aon lionn Oub ná póncar eile
Seáca San Séamuis Áz Cliaż

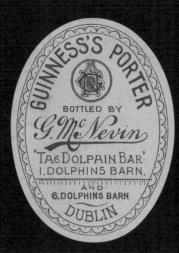

GUINNESS'S PORTER
BOTTLED BY
G. McNevin
"Tae Dolpain Bar"
1, DOLPHINS BARN,
AND
6, DOLPHINS BARN
DUBLIN

GUINNESS
STOUT
CERVEZA GUINNESS CABEZA DE PERRO
FORTALECE
DOG'S HEAD
BOTTLING

GUINNESS'S PORTER
BOTTLED BY
JAMES HEFFERNAN
103,
SOUTH CIRCULAR RD.
DUBLIN

GUINNESS'S
George F. Hewett Co
Bottled Expressly
FOR
GEO. F. HEWETT CO.,
BOSTON
U.S.A.
EXTRA FOREIGN STOUT

GUINNESS'S EXTRA STOUT
TRADE MARK.
BOTTLED EXPRESSLY BY
C. MACHEN & HUDSON
LIVERPOOL
LION BRAND

GUINNESS'S STOUT
JUSTICE FREEDOM
COMMERCE
FINEST PROCURABLE

W.E. JOHNSON & CO.
TRADE MARK
GUINNESS'S STOUT
BOTTLED EXPRESSLY FOR EXPORTATION
NONE GENUINE
WITHOUT
TRADE MARK
ON LABEL AND
CAPSULE.
LIVERPOOL

GUINNESS'S
WHITE STAR
BRAND
SOLD
ALL OVER
THE
WORLD
EXTRA · FOREIGN · STOUT

railway wagons and road transport for delivery of beer to the city and country. Guinness retired its last horse in 1960 finally putting to an end a mode of transport that had lasted for over 200 years.

Throughout this time the brewery was expanding rapidly to meet demand for its unique stouts. 1873 saw the greatest expansion both in buildings for increased production and in land area, which was needed to facilitate this growth. In that year Guinness expanded north across James's Street to take over an area of some 12 hectares, all the way to the banks of the Liffey. This created what was termed the *Upper Level* and *Lower Level* zones within the brewery. To reorganize the process of brewing, several departments were moved to the new lower level zone including the cooperage or barrel making along with the cask washing and filling facilities. However, it became more and more difficult to move materials around the much larger site with horsepower alone.

Above

Light, cameras... action

The barges offered a unique perspective of the river and city. Film crews were eager to exploit this new platform and Guinness were happy to oblige. Here a film crew shoots scenes close to St. Paul's Church on Arran Quay in the 1950s.

Images on this page courtesy of Guinness Archives

The Company's solution was to construct a narrow gauge railway, not only within the complex but also underneath it too. This connected both levels and at its completion in 1877 the railway ran for a distance of more than 12 kilometres. The major problem facing the engineers at the time centred around connecting the two levels which were around 15 metres apart in height. The solution was to use the Alpine method of tunnelling where a circular section of the railway turned 2.5 times at a radius of over

Above

Victoria Quay

The first set of barges Guinness built were all named after Irish rivers and are seen here, fully loaded and ready to depart downriver.

18 metres to connect both upper and lower level tracks under James's Street.

The first five engines were steam powered and delivered between 1875 and 1878. These didn't prove entirely practical due to a lack of grit and dirt protection, which duly affected their performance. So the Head Engineer of the brewery, Samuel Geoghegan set about designing and constructing an engine that could overcome these deficiencies. This new steam engine proved to be such an outright success that the company ordered another seventeen. These were used to haul the malt wagons, spent grain, casks, hops and other materials from the upper to lower levels and vice versa. If proof was needed for their effectiveness then the very fact that they lasted in service right up to and after the Second World War was proof of good design along with sound materials and construction methods. Diesels took over after 1947 and 12 were purchased for work right up to the railway's retirement in 1975.

In May 1769, just ten years after opening the brewery Guinness exported his first barrels of stout - half a dozen of them, to Britain. An inauspicious start maybe to the tidal waves of stout that was to be exported over the coming centuries. Guinness made good use of the Grand Canal when it first opened in the late 18th century to transport the growing number of barrels, down to the Dublin Port for shipment overseas. The horse-drawn barges on the canal took most of the day to get down to the port having to navigate several sets of locks on their way to the waiting ships. The horses too were not built for speed so a leisurely pace was maintained. Only with the opening of the brewery's lower level zone in 1873 that brought the new boundary right up to the banks of the river Liffey that a new chapter in water borne transport began.

Below

Opening Act

Toucans made their first appearance in Guinness advertising in 1935. Dreamt up by the famous English artist John Gilroy they were last used in 2005 when Guinness closed the Park Royal brewery in London and returned to Dublin.

With their contrasting colours and humourous demeanour they quickly gained the public's recognition and appeared in a variety of situations over the intervening years.

Images on these pages courtesy of Guinness Archives

Guinness realized quickly that the Liffey also offered much more room, capacity and speed for even larger barges to be built and used to transport the casks downriver to the port. Victoria Quay was specially constructed in 1873 outside the boundary of the brewery for this very task and the first barges now powered by steam were being built at the

Preceding pages
**Loading Guinness
on the Liffey, Dublin**

*Oil on canvas - 1955
76 x 102 cms*

by **Terence Cuneo**

Below

Guinness Sign

Guinness produced a
raft of merchandising
material which included
this enamelled sign for
outside pubs.

Right

**Guinness Barge
passing under the
Ha'penny Bridge**

Guinness barges always
attracted attention
whenever they took to
the river. Here a group
of children watch with
rapt attention as one of
the barges passes under
the bridge as it travels
back to the brewery.

*Images on this page
courtesy of Guinness Archives*

same time. This set of barges were named after Irish rivers so names such as
Foyle, Shannon, Moy, Slaney, Dodder and *Liffey* became commonplace as they
slowly chugged up and down the river. Upon arriving downriver the barges
would be met by ships who would take on board the full casks of Guinness and
transfer the returning empty ones.

The first of these was built by Harland & Wolff in Belfast and was named *Lagan*
after the river that flows through that city. The second was called *Shannon* and
was built in Preston, England while the next ten that followed were all built by
Ross & Walpole in Dublin. The barges, *Liffey* and *Boyne* were commandeered

by the British Army during the First World War and saw service on French
canals before being returned after the War's end. *Tolka* was the last to be built
in Dublin and was called the Motor Boat as she had a petrol engine to drive
her instead of steam. But each of these barges had similar carrying capacities
of some 240 hogsheads (1 Hogshead equalled 54 imperial gallons).

By the early 20th century Guinness was acknowledged to be the largest brewery in the world, due primarily to a thriving export trade. From 1769 onwards the brewery had used the services of various shipping companies and agents to deliver its product overseas. This changed in 1913 when Guinness set about building of its very own fleet of ships with the arrival of the *W M Barkley*, a steam ship of some 600 tons. This was followed by nine other ships of various tonnages that served primarily on the Dublin to Liverpool and Manchester routes.

Guinness had a huge bottling operation in Liverpool especially setup for the export trade and Liverpool was one of Britain's largest ports at the time with frequent sailings to the rest of the world. The Guinness fleet would go on to operate for over eighty years and its ships, with dark blue hulls and a cream superstructure became a familiar sight in these ports. The last ship of the line was the *Miranda Guinness* of some 1500 tons which was the world's first specially commissioned bulk liquid beer carrier with a capacity of nearly two million pints.

The arrival of ever larger and more roll-on roll-off ferries in Dublin in the latter years of the 20th century signaled the end for the Guinness fleet. With their frequent sailings and reduced rates Guinness opted to use large stainless steel road tankers for overseas bulk delivery. The two remaining ships in service, the *Lady Patricia* and the *Miranda Guinness* made their last voyages in 1993 when the brewery's shipping service was discontinued.

Model of a Guinness Barge

The barges were shallow and wide and designed to specifically navigate the Liffey and the city's bridges at high tide.

Photograph by the Author

When Victoria Quay was first opened it had capacity for three berths. This was increased by 1892 to six and by 1913 there were eleven berths - five for emptying and six for loading. Barrels of stout from the brewery were delivered by the narrow gauge railway, which crossed the quay road to the waiting 'Lighters' as they were referred to.

Opposite

The Guinness Brewery

Lithograph
c.1880/90s

Artist unknown

But the Liffey was also a tidal river from the King's Bridge, just west of Guinness to the sea and so a new set of operational procedures would have to be implemented. As the barges were now larger they could only move at high tide with a full load of barrels on board. This necessitated moving downstream in convoys at different times during the day and also at night. Once they'd transferred their load of full barrels to the ships the barges would be filled with empty ones for the return journey to Victoria Quay at the next high tide. In the 1920s it was reported that virtually every day at least eight fully loaded barges set off from Victoria Quay for the port, 2.5 kilometres away. One of the many bridges that the barges passed under was of course the Ha'penny Bridge.

Above

Double Act

Guinness advertising featured a menagerie of different animals over a number of decades.

Sea lions were chosen for this particular poster by John Gilroy because of their free-spirited and playful nature, .

Images on these pages courtesy of Guinness Archives

Children standing on the bridge with their heads poking through the railings would shout to the crews below... 'Hey Mister, bring us back a parrot' along no doubt, with other colourful requests believing the crews on board, would be heading for more exotic destinations all over the world.

During the War of Independence from 1920 - 21 Dublin was under curfew at night and special passes were issued to the Guinness boatmen to

The Harp

The harp is the historic symbol of the island of Ireland having been recognised and officially used since the late 11th and early 12th centuries.

To this day Guinness and the Republic of Ireland both use the harp as their official symbols. The designs are both based on the famous 14th century 'Brian Boru' harp which is now preserved in the Library of Trinity College, Dublin.

Images on these pages courtesy of Guinness Archives

The harp was first used as a symbol on bottles of Guinness in 1862. Here is the classic label, oval in shape with plain black lettering on a sandy, buff base.

This label was produced in the company's plant in Liverpool for stout exported overseas.

operate the barges inside the curfew hours as the hourly operations at Victoria Quay were constantly changing due to the tides. In May 1921 the Custom House was set on fire, which hampered Guinness's operations, as this was where much of the export barrels were stored prior to shipment overseas. Alternative arrangements were quickly in place and operations continued in what must have been a fraught atmosphere.

In 1922 during the Civil War that followed, the Four Courts came under sustained attack from the Free State Army who bombarded the Anti-Treaty forces who had occupied it. Even these actions didn't stop the sailings of these craft. While the Captain stayed on deck, often risking small arms fire and sniping the crew took cover below and were paid danger money for their trouble. Stories like this and others of barges being swept from their moorings during heavy floods and causing some chaos in the river downstream abound. Another recounts a fully loaded barge being swamped by waves from a strong easterly wind and sinking at Custom House Quay. Because of this the barrels from the open hold floated off down the river and the remaining barges swept the port, managing to retrieve around half the load. For weeks after casks were reported to be washing up on beaches up and down the East coast. But every cask when returned - as they were, was empty.

In 1927 after nearly 50 years of continuous service these barges were withdrawn and replaced by a new set of ten barges called the 'Farmleigh' type. These barges were built downstream in the port at the Vickers owned Liffey Dockyard. They were again steam driven but with several improvements for the crews that served on them. For a start they were easier to manoeuvre in the river and now the crews also had better accommodation below deck. The first barge was called *Farmleigh* after the Guinness family home close to the Phoenix Park. The rest followed until 1931 with names such as *Castlenock, Killiney, Sandyford* and other Dublin place names. Their top speed of 7.5 knots brought them from

Guinness's to Dublin Port in around 20 minutes, a vast improvement over the times of the first barges on the Grand Canal.

Their overall length of 24.5 metres and a 5 metre width meant they could now carry some 90-100 tons of beer or 300 hogsheads of Guinness. Each barge or lighter had a Captain, Mate, Engine driver and two Boatsmen. The elegantly dressed Captain in dark blue corduroys, a shiny peaked cap and a heavy dark blue jersey with *GUINNESS* embroidered on the front in red. These boats also had funnels that had to be lowered when going under the several stone bridges at high tide. The only bridge where they didn't need to do this was the Ha'penny Bridge.

A crew of up to twelve men handled work on Victoria Quay in the early 1930s and they could load around one thousand casks in a single shift. But one thousand, five hundred casks were often loaded in twelve hours, which wasn't unusual either. With the opening of the new Guinness brewery at Park Royal outside London to service parts of the UK market in 1936 and the introduction of more and more lorries, loads carried by

Guinness first used the harp symbol back in 1862 on a bottle and had trademarked it by 1876. The first Irish Free State Government of 1922 also chose the harp to be the new country's official symbol, cognisant of its role in the past.

Both Guinness and the Irish Free State later came to an agreement so that both could use the harp, but facing alternate directions.

Over the years there have been a number of changes to the design of the Guinness harp as it was modernised and simplified and included a gradual reduction in the number of strings.

| 1862 | 1955 | 1968 | 1997 | 2005 | 2016 |

the barges began to decline. By 1938 only six of the ten remained in service. The advent of the World War II caught Guinness on the hop as fuel became expensive and scarce. Coal of the lowest quality called 'duff' and wood scraps however remained available, which gave the barges a more important role in the distribution chain. Here too, one of the Guinness barges *Fairyhouse* made it across the Irish Sea and up the English Channel in 1939 to assist in the evacuation of an allied army

The new harp, (above) introduced in 2016 marks a return to a more traditional harp and is now three dimensional.

The Irish State however continues to use the original harp (similar in style to the 1955 version) without modification.

Above
Guinness Tanker
Photograph - 2015
by **Kevin Griffin**
Guinness still makes its
way down the Liffey to
the port in specially
fabricated road tankers.

This publicity photo
humourously takes this
to the next level with a
giant 500ml can of the
black stuff superimposed
onto a truck and trailer
with the brewery in the
background.

Courtesy of the Artist

trapped on the beaches of Dunkirk. After the war had ended the Lighters' role diminished even further and the few remaining sailed on into the early 1960s. The last of these barges made its final voyage on 21 June 1961 and this along the rest of the fleet were sold and sailed to other parts of the country and Britain. The dock at Victoria Quay was removed some time after this but it didn't stop Guinness from transporting its beer down the old route of the Liffey.

Guinness is still widely enjoyed in Ireland and another 150 countries around the world and is one of the country's strongest and most important exports. To this day it still travels down the Liffey from the very same brewery first opened more than 250 years ago - albeit in specially made chrome plated road tankers to Dublin Port. There it is driven onto fast, frequent ferries that convey the precious cargo to the United Kingdom and a myriad of other countries further afield.

Over their significant lifetimes both Guinness and the Ha'penny Bridge have become two of the most recognized icons of the city of Dublin. Together they have lent their unique history, heritage and culture along with their stability and permanence to a city that's always expanding, evolving and progressing. These two charismatic structures, one a colossus on the world stage and at the very forefront of a global industry - the other a simple pedestrian bridge, diminutive in size that conveys thousands every day back and forth across the Liffey. That both are now the most visited sites on any Dublin '*to-do*' list speaks volumes for their joint overall stature and appeal, worldwide. Not to mention the growing global audience eager to experience both.

Below

Balancing Act

The toucans make their final exit.

Image courtesy of Guinness Archives

The Song of Zozimus

by Michael J. Moran 'Zozimus'

Gather round me boys, will yez
Gather round me?
And hear what I have to say,
Before ould Sally brings me
My bread and jug of tay.

I live in Faddle Alley,
Off Blackpitts near the Coombe;
With my poor wife called Sally,
in a narrow, dirty room.

Gather round me, and stop yer noise,
Gather round me till my tale is told;
Gather round me, ye girls and ye boys,
Till I tell yez stories of the days of old;
Gather round me, all ye ladies fair,
And ye gentlemen of renown;
Listen, listen, and to me repair,
While I sing of beauteous Dublin town.

Preceding pages
A winter's evening on the Liffey Boardwalk

Opposite
Surface wake

Following pages
The southern end of Liffey Street

All photographs by the Author

Part of Dublin's cultural quarter

5

Part of Dublin's cultural quarter

by Annette Black

Co-Author of *The Bridges of Dublin*

hen, in May 1816, Dubliners strolled across the Ha'penny Bridge for the very first time a mere six other bridges straddled the Liffey within the city. Looking baywards to where O'Connell Bridge now stands, was Gandon's humpbacked Carlisle Bridge of 1794, cluttered by tall ships' masts on the seaward side and already crumbling under the dense weight of trundling 19th century traffic. On the quaysides urchin children playing 'hoop-la' vied for space with sailors and cattle drovers, apple sellers and merchants.

To the west was Essex Bridge, completed in 1755 to the design of self-taught engineer George Semple and funded by one guinea lottery tickets. Narrow and steep, it led from fashionable Capel Street lined with Dutch style mansions to the Royal Exchange (City Hall) where wily merchants brokered deals, and to the very seat of power itself - Dublin Castle.

It wouldn't be replaced by Grattan's Bridge for another 50 years.

Beyond, where the craggy remains of the 17th century Ormonde Bridge had doggedly stood since it was washed away by ferocious Liffey floods in 1802, was now the beautiful, stone built, three arched Richmond Bridge (O'Donovan Rossa Bridge), declared open on St. Patrick's Day 1816. Lawyers, in flurries of gowns and wigs, weaved back and forth across the bridge as they went about their business beneath the grand dome of the Four Courts.

And between there and the Queen's Bridge of 1768 (Mellows Bridge) where charity collectors rattle wooden boxes under your nose and occasional screams floated across the river from the correctional house, the Bridewell, the construction of yet another bridge (Father Mathew Bridge) was underway to replace 'that crazy, wretched pile of antiquity' – the Old Bridge of 1428.

On the city horizon, was the 'rude' looking Barrack Bridge of 1700, a tottering four arch, stone structure grandiosely embellished by the castellated Richmond Tower. Beyond the fashionable reach of the city

Opposite

Halfpenny Bridge

Oil on canvas - 2007
100 x 120cm

by **Martin Stone**
Courtesy of the Artist

Left

An early representation of the bridge

This is one of the first illustrations of the bridge produced for an avid public, curious to see what the cast iron footbridge looked like.

The bridge has been deliberately enhanced with a sharper incline to make it look higher and also by picturing it at low tide.

Courtesy of Dublin City Council

it was favoured by oft unruly soldiers from the nearby Royal Barracks (Collins Barracks), street vendors and market gardeners from the surrounding countryside and those with a trick to turn on the city streets.

Dubliners, it seems, had every reason to welcome the city's first ever pedestrian only bridge. It was a new bridge for new times.

Not forgotten by city folk was 1798 when the rebels were hung from the bridges and cartloads of broken bodies, in tell-tale brown peasant coats, came into the city under cover of darkness for burial in the riverside Croppies Acre. Indeed, one of the names bestowed by Dubliners on the bridge would recall this bloody episode in Irish history: the Triangle Bridge referred to a cruel punishment meted out to rebels by one of the bridge's promoters. John Claudius Beresford, parliamentarian, tortured rebels upon a triangular scaffold in his Dublin riding school.

Robert Emmet's doomed rebellion of 1803, when mayhem broke loose on the streets of Dublin and Emmet was barbarically hanged, drawn and quartered in full public gaze still haunted Dubliners. They were reeling too from the recent loss of the Irish Parliament, following the Act of Union of 1800. In the years that followed the political and titled classes abandoned the city for the greater promise offered by London. Dublin was still the second city of the British Empire but had already begun its inexorable slide to mere fifth place by 1900.

And, in 1816, the payment of a toll was nothing new for Dublin bridge users – even desirable if one wanted to keep their distance from the poorer class of folk.

Thus, a watercolour drawing of 1818 (pages 58/59) depicts the Ha'penny Bridge at the centre of a most desirable, Georgian, urban idyll - the newly opened, elegant bridge at the heart of an elegant city, with an elegantly dressed population strolling by. The bridge, a simple feat of engineering beauty, springs lightly across the river, even the well-proportioned, dome topped toll booths at each end of the bridge did not distract from its graceful appearance.

And then there was the convenience. The bridge offered easy access from the then fashionable northside to the popular Crow Street theatre where world famous actors treaded the boards. Ferries had plied their trade on this stretch of water since time immemorial but a dip in the icy, none too clean, water was not an unusual outcome. What was a ha'penny to those who could pay five shillings for a gallery seat or an outrageous half a guinea for a box?

The bridge arrived on full-masted sailing ships direct from the Coalbrookdale Foundry in England and spectators came from all over Ireland to witness its erection on site. Not only was it the first iron bridge for the city it was one of the very few in the industrialising world. Officially 'Wellington Bridge', named for Arthur Wellesley the first Duke of Wellington, the hero of Waterloo in 1815. Commander in Chief of the British Army and two time Prime Minister of Great Britain - his fellow Dubliners with little else at their command, rejected this imperial moniker in favour of the Metal Bridge and immortalised as such in James Joyce's *Ulysses*, that meandering, chronicle of the world's most famous pedestrian, Leopold Bloom. Lenehan, the not so lucky racing editor at a Dublin newspaper and the unshaven McCoy... 'crossed to the Metal Bridge and and went along Wellington Quay by the river wall.'

By times it was also the Iron Bridge, the cruelly evocative, Triangle Bridge but most memorably the Ha'penny Bridge.

The 19th century brought unequal measures of despair and hope to an ever expanding Dublin. Daniel O'Connell and his very modern mass movement for political change gave repressed Catholics hope and vital progress with Catholic emancipation granted in 1829. Hopes rose and fell again with failed rebellions in 1848 and 1867. The country wide Great Famine in mid-century saw the starved and wretched limp into the city seeking salvation or emigration. The Ha'penny Bridge became a symbol of remembrance, featuring on a *Carte de Visite* for the emigrant, available from Burkes, by the Metal Bridge for 6 pence.

And as the industrial revolution progressed there grew a city of two parts – desperate poverty in overcrowded, crumbling mansions, characterised by open cess pits in the gardens and deserted by the wealthier who, with the advent of the railway, took to the suburbs. The elegant Georgian city entered a period of long, existential struggle. The romantic Ha'penny Bridge gave way to the utilitarian one – and what better use to put it to than a convenient advertising billboard?

A grainy, black and white photo of the late 19th century reveals a work-a-day city, the Ha'penny Bridge having become somewhat of a municipal washing line:

Adhesive Sticker

Carrolls Irish Gifts

Small Dish

Mullingar Pewter

A marketeer's dream

The Ha'penny Bridge is now one of the most recognised icons of the city of Dublin.

As such it features on a bewildering array of products not only for the home market but also for visitors eager to grab a souvenir. While many of these are of the cheap and cheerful variety, many others display a more contemporary and stylistic approach.

Photographs by the Author
Products displayed are courtesy of the providers.

Ceramic Plate

Carrolls Irish Gifts

Pub Logo

Ha'penny Bridge Inn

Dubin Canvas Bag

Carrolls Irish Gifts

Liffey Players Logo

Theatre Group, Alberta, Canada

Tracing your Dublin Ancestors

Flyleaf Press

T Shirt

Carrolls Irish Gifts

Dublin Holly Bag

Robin-Ruth

Fridge magnet

Carrolls Irish Gifts

If Ever You Go

Dedalus Press

Fridge magnet

Carrolls Irish Gifts

Milk Carton

Premier Dairies

Picture Frame

Mullingar Pewter

Bronze Token

Carrolls Irish Gifts

Products not
to scale

Pocket purse

Carrolls Irish Gifts

20 things to do in Dublin...

O'Brien Press

Brass Bottle Opener

Carrolls Irish Gifts

Whiskey Flask

Carrolls Irish Gifts

Europa Stamp

An Post

Below right

The bridge in music

Over the years various musicians and bands including U2 have used the bridge as a back-drop in photographs and videos to promote their music.

Phil Lynott - one of Ireland's most charismatic performers appeared in a video for his single 'Old Town' that featured the Ha'penny Bridge prominently.

Phil Lynott continues to receive acclaim long after his premature death in 1986. A poster for a commemorative concert 'The Sun Goes Down' was issued in 2016.

Poster design by Robbie Bray and Smiley Bolger and courtesy of the artists.

Far right

The bridge was again the centre of attention when a lavish musical, set in 1916 and written by Alastair McGuckian was staged in Dublin in 2005. The production was generally well received by audiences who saw it but critics were less enthusiastic with the production that featured a populist story line set amidst the backdrop of the Easter Rebellion.

Image courtesy of Simon Roche

French's Epilepsy Remedy (page 7) – each giant letter, running south to north, spelt out hope for a little understood affliction on the eastern side of the bridge. The northside toll booth has disappeared giving the bridge a lopsided look and a clutter of notice boards at each end of the bridge disfigure its clear lines.

At some point the toll – for those rushing back and forth to the antique shops, biscuit and starch warehouses, prayer halls, shirt factories and abstinence societies on the north and south quays - was raised to a penny ha'penny, the price of three bread buns as the 19th century turned to the 20th. Weary Dubliners, with little enough bread to fill the mouths of their large families, stuck with the more economical Ha'penny name.

An 1897 letter to the editor of *The Irish Times* pleaded with Dublin Corporation to get rid of the toll – there were often traffic jams at each foot of the bridge as people waited to pay and this interfered with traffic. In addition, O'Connell and Grattan Bridges were overrun with those avoiding the toll – somewhat a badge of honour for some Dubliners! According to Dr. David Clare, theatre historian, it amused the playwright George Bernard Shaw to tell of his father shouting 'This infernal bridge will break me!' as he strode across - one less

for John Huston with admiration affection and thanks   donal 2·25·'87

ha'penny in his never full enough pockets and only the gulls' plaintive cries in response. But, even as the 19th century turned to the 20th, the bridge did not belong to the city. The lease was still held in private and the tolls accrued to individuals. About this time Dubliners liked to call it the Rainbow Bridge – there was a pot of gold at each end! The native Dublin wit also relished the challenge of getting the better of any type of establishment setup. A popular ruse was for two people to present to the toll keeper. One would pose an innocent question: 'Is there any charge for what you might carry on you back?' Upon hearing the required answer – 'No' – the second man would hop on the back of the first, pay a single toll and gallop across the bridge.

Where comedy plays, tragedy soon follows. On Easter Tuesday, 1916, as the Rising burst upon the city, one young man, James Crawford Neil, a junior member of staff in the National Library, made the fateful decision to avoid the shooting on O'Connell Bridge. As the 24 years

old breadwinner for a large family headed by his widowed mother crossed the Ha'penny bridge a single shot rang out and he fell, mortally wounded.

1916 was also the year in which the bridge's lease finally reverted to Dublin Corporation, though the last toll was collected by Mr. Booth, the toll keeper, three years later. Through the years of war that followed the city did not have much to celebrate – mere survival was at stake. If money was spent on the city's architectural treasures it was done so to rebuild the Custom House, Four Courts and General Post Office, though in a flurry of patriotic renaming in 1923 Wellington Bridge officially became the 'Liffey Bridge'. Stubborn Dubliners took no note nor showed any attachment to the now garish bridge with unpainted hoardings and worn out footways. 'Was it to remain in this condition', asked another letter to the editor, 'until a new bridge is constructed?'

The early years of the 20th century were bleak with 1929 providing one highlight – the celebration of 100 years of Catholic emancipation. The Ha'penny Bridge once more functioned as a notice board with '1829 – 1929' hung from the bridge railings below a large cross.

Photos of the 1940s depict the bridge denuded of garish advertising hoardings and unsightly notice boards, but looking care worn and faded with gap-toothed and paint chipped railings.

Other mid-century photos show flag pole extension poles lifted the advertising over and above the profile of the bridge, destroying any remaining vestiges of its elegant design. Though blackened by the smog of the city and the puffs of smoke from the Guinness barges chugging beneath, it provided a fine spot from which children could peer through the railings and watch the shoals of mullet come in on the tide.

From time to time the public were treated to various schemes to replace the bridge. The earliest of these was in 1913 when Sir Hugh Lane, art collector, proposed an elaborate structure including gallery and promenades and designed by Edwin Lutyens. Dublin Corporation adopted the proposal but in a fit of infighting reneged on the deal, citing Lutyens being only half Irish and this did not compensate for

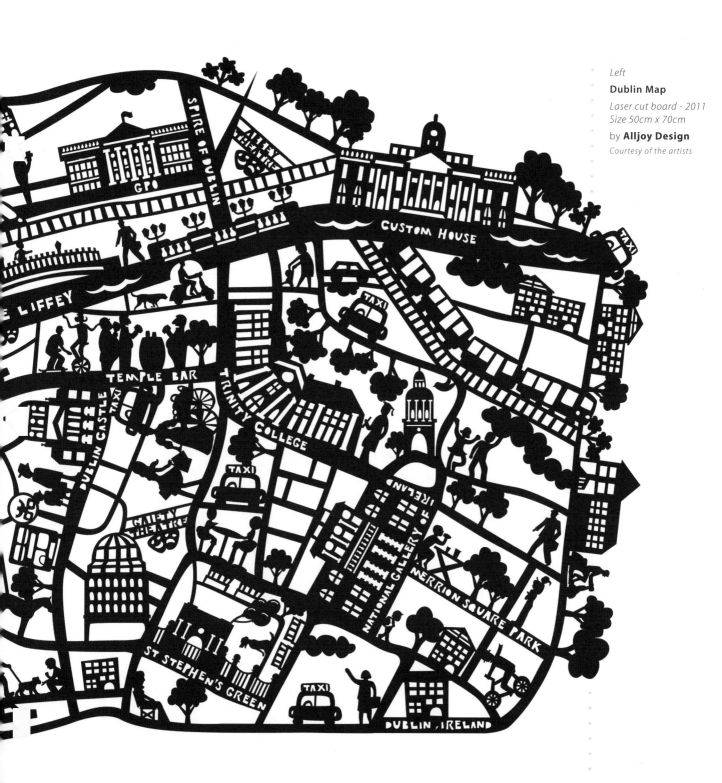

Left

Dublin Map
Laser cut board - 2011
Size 50cm x 70cm

by **Alljoy Design**
Courtesy of the artists

171

his being half English. A mid-century proposal sought to replace the bridge with a road bridge and a later proposal envisaged the paving over of the river at this location for use as a car park. The bridge fell in and out of use as an advertising billboard, sometimes appealing to Dubliners to buy Spratt's Patent Dog Cakes and at other times Fry's Chocolate (pages 71/89). It was painted in shades of green, silver, black and at other times not painted at all. The wooden deck was covered with unsightly tarmac and the historic surrounding area fell into disrepair - where lively Temple Bar now stands a central bus station was very nearly built.

Whatever the bridge lacked in personality through these years, Dubliners provided in spades. The bridge became a place of three card tricks, accordion players, the music hall sales pitch of Mr. Hector Grey ringing across the bridge exhorting all "Me auld flowers... leave the carbolic and sunlight soap for the gurriers and try the secrets of Mandarin Soap. Four shillings in Harrods but two bob here."

Opposite and left

A magnet for poverty

The ongoing issues surrounding destitute people forced to beg on Dublin's streets shows no sign of abating. The focus of this humiliating exercise is played out daily on the Ha'penny Bridge and other areas of the city centre.

Poverty brought on by a range of social issues including: alcohol and drug addiction; loss of employment; the break up of marriage or eviction from home and family. These and other factors force these people to congregate here and eke out the most basic of existences.

Life on the streets offers little protection to vulnerable people locked in a constant spiral of despair, protecting what little they have. The lack of even basic living standards can lead to further depressive tendencies which are difficult to reconcile.

Social services and charities dedicated to providing food and shelter offer some hope but for the most part these people go unnoticed by citizens who just pass them by.

Photograph by the Author

Opposite

Ciarán Keogh and Azzurra Damen during the Dublin Simon Community soup run in November 2012.

Photographer: Dara Mac Donaill/The Irish Times

Hector Grey's Shop

Hector Grey was a Dublin institution and an important cog of the retail and social fabric of the city.

One of his shops was on Liffey Street close to the Ha'penny Bridge. This sold a huge range of bric-a-brac and every-day items that Dublin shoppers willingly hoovered up.

But they also came for something else - Street Theatre. A gifted speaker and charismatic racon-teur Grey entertained the crowds with words of wisdom, scandal, satire and sales patter which made this unique shopping experience all the more entertaining.

Courtesy of Dublin City Council

By the 1990s the bridge was a sad sight indeed and from time to time Dubliners implored the Corporation through letters to the editors of national newspapers. A Mr. Trout pleaded for a facelift and new lighting scheme for the bridge.

Salvation came in 2001 with the major refurbishment of the bridge. It now adorns the river, suitably sparling like the jewel it is. A rainbow bridge for a rainbow city.

Below left

The bridge's 200th Anniversary Celebrations

The Lord Mayor, Criona Ni Daliagh makes her speech while Gardai clear the bridge prior to the official walk-over with invited dignitaries.

Above

Later... Dubliners and visitors get to sample the red carpet treatment themselves and pose for photographs.

Photographs by the Author

Ha'penny Bridge

by Pat Boran

Collecting coppers on an Irish Flag —
a spectre in a 'Simpsons' sleeping bag.

Down by the Liffeyside

by Peadar Kearney

Twas down by Anna Liffey, my love and I did stray
Where in the good old slushy mud the sea gulls sport and play.
We got the whiff of ray and chips and Mary softly sighed,
"Oh John, come on for a wan and wan
Down by the Liffeyside."

Then down along by George's Street the loving pairs to view,
While Mary swanked it like a queen in a skirt of royal blue;
Her hat was lately turned and her blouse was newly dyed,
Oh you could not match her round the block,
Down by the Liffeyside.

And on her old melodeon how sweetly could she play
'Good-by-ee' and 'Don't sigh-ee' and 'Rule Brittanni-ay.'
But when she turned Sinn Feiner me heart near burst with pride,
To hear her sing 'The Soldier's Song,'
Down by the Liffeyside.

On Sunday morning to Meath Street together we will go,
And it's up to Father Murphy we both will make our vow.
We'll join our hands in wedlock bands and we'll be soon outside
For a whole afternoon, for our honeymoon,
Down by the Liffeyside.

Preceding pages

The bridge in 1973

Ireland is now is enjoying a level of prosperity after years of austerity and this is reflected in the buildup of traffic on the quays. Much of it is private and this along with commercial traffic is now routed up and down the quays in new one-way systems. This was later reversed in 1982 to the current setup with traffic heading out of town on the south quays, while traffic entering the city did so along the north quays. Compare this photograph with the one on pages 68/69.

Also of note are the array of high antennas erected to amplify the weak signals of British radio and television stations, which were generally unavailable to Irish audiences at the time.

Courtesy of Dublin City Council

Opposite page

Window shopping

The Dublin Woollen Mills occupied this corner site of Liffey Street from the 1930s onwards selling a comprehensive range of Irish made fashions.
It finally closed its doors in 2012 and has now been transformed into a food shop and restaurant.

Photograph by the Author

A new
lease of life

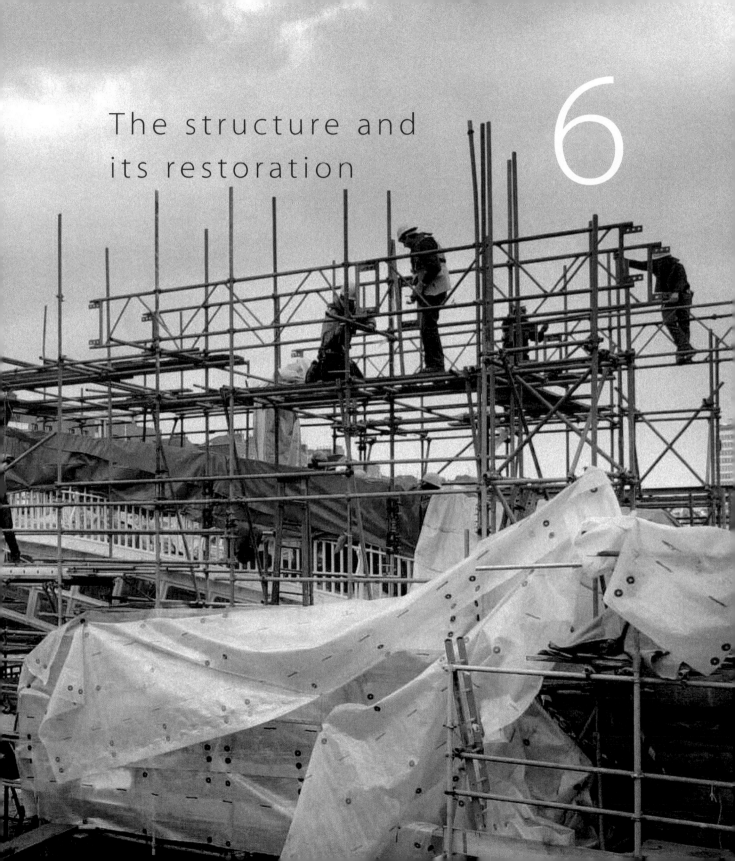

The structure and
its restoration

6

The structure and its restoration

by Michael B. Barry

Co-Author of *The Bridges of Dublin*

Preceding pages

The wraps come off

Workmen complete the task of removing the last of the scaffolding and protective sheeting from around the restored structure in 2001.

Courtesy of Dublin City Council

Opposite

The bridge from Merchants Arch

Pedestrians make their way through the arch on a bright, winter morning.

Photograph by the Author

he Ha'penny Bridge in Dublin was a pioneering structure. The use of cast iron was a new technique in the construction of bridges, previously made from masonry or timber. It was Dublin's (and Ireland's) first bridge using the new material of cast iron and was followed rapidly by the King's Bridge of 1829 (adjacent to Heuston Station). It was unique in world terms – few cast iron bridges had been made by that stage. The bridge led the way in another sense: it was the first pedestrian bridge to be erected over the Liffey in Dublin.

Previously ferries had shuttled people over the river at this point. Clearly a bridge has greater capacity, is easier and less hazardous than a ferry. As the Georgian city had developed rapidly on both sides of the Liffey during the great period of 18th century growth, the volume of traffic across the river had built up. There was an obvious need for a bridge. In an early example of Public Private Partnership (PPP), William Walsh, who operated the decaying ferries, decided that he would replace these

Above

Showing its age

Temporary measures are undertaken to reinforce the dilapidated structure prior to its restoration.

Photograph courtesy of Paul Arnold Architects

with a footbridge. In March 1815, he gathered political support and presented a proposal for a metal-arched footbridge, to the 'Corporation for the Preservation and Improvement of the Port of Dublin'. He also attached detailed plans by the Coalbrookdale iron foundry in Shropshire, which had built the world's first iron bridge. The Corporation called in various experts to assess the proposal, including the prominent architect Francis Johnston as well as John Semple (son of George Semple who had built Essex Bridge and had written *A Treatise on Building in Water*). Favourable reports were given and Walsh was given permission to build his bridge. To finance it, he had a 99-year lease for the operation of the bridge toll. The toll was not to exceed a halfpenny, that being the toll charged on the ferry.

It was most likely economics, not aestheticism that was the driving force in choosing a metal bridge. (However, as it happens, the resulting Ha'penny Bridge scored highly on aesthetics). Constructing a masonry-arched bridge was a tried and tested method. However, precisely cutting stone, placing this and erecting the bridge would have required much time from skilled tradesmen, mainly stone masons. It would also have required a pier in the river. All of this would be costly. It is likely that a cast-iron bridge would be quicker and less expensive. The design, casting and construction of these iron bridges had been much improved since the erection of the world's first iron bridge in Shropshire in 1779. Even today, PPP contractors seek out the less expensive solution: look at the West-Link and East-Link bridges, where cost considerations outweighed aesthetics. The contract for the bridge was placed, around April 1815 (two months before the Battle of Waterloo) with the Coalbrookdale Iron Foundry, owned by Abraham Darby III. One account says that the cost was £3,000. It also states that John Windsor, a foreman at the foundry, was the designer.

Precise measurements would have been made at the site on the Liffey and details of the required span and rise (to allow river navigation) of the bridge would have been sent to Coalbrookdale. The foundry experts would have drawn up the details of the structure, including a side elevation of the bridge (maybe marking it out on the ground), thus allowing them to identify and specify the precise dimensions of the individual members. The intricate connections would have been ascertained. Moulds were

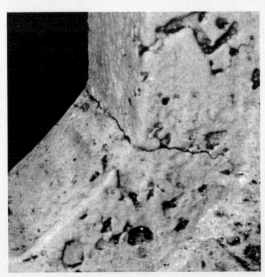

then made of the complex series of components making up the bridge. The molten iron was poured into the moulds, and when cooled the moulds were removed. The cast iron members would be examined, any burrs filed off and the requisite holes drilled at connection points. It is highly probable that there was a trial assembly of some or all of the structure at the foundry, before dispatch. It would not have done to send it to Dublin and discover there that the bridge would not fit together. Anyone with experience of erecting a steel bridge knows that it is never a perfect world when trying to fit things together. A sledge hammer plus a steel bar, is very helpful in ensuring things fit. However, while one might be able to do this with steel which is flexible, one could not with the more brittle cast iron. Hence the need to ensure everything fitted together, before it was shipped to Dublin.

The finished cast iron members were then transported by barge down the River Severn to the Bristol Channel, where it would be transhipped to a sailing vessel for onward journey to

Above

Temporary fix

This image shows how the original diagonal bracing members on the left hand side were cut away on the right and replaced with ugly tubular steel members.

During the restoration these were replaced with new cast iron members fabricated in the original style.

*Photograph courtesy of
Paul Arnold Architects*

Dublin. It would then have been unloaded at the Dublin quays, as the Carlisle (now O'Connell) Bridge of 1794 would have prevented the cross-channel vessel from proceeding to the bridge site. The iron sections were transported to the site either by road or by barge. The granite bridge abutments being completed, it is likely that falsework centring was erected across the river, with support members down to the river bed, in a similar fashion as in the construction of a masonry-arch bridge. The temporary timberwork (page 61) would be in the shape of the soffit of the bridge. Workmen (probably under the supervision of an expert from Coalbrookdale), put the cast-iron members in place, across the span. These would have been fitted together and then bolted. When the structure was complete, the timber centring would be removed. A timber decking was fixed to allow for pedestrian traffic. The final part in the sequence would have been a load test. Usually a squad of soldiers would march over, testing the performance of the bridge, to prove that it would not collapse! Demonstrating the speed of construction of a cast iron bridge in comparison to a masonry arch one, the bridge was formally opened on 19 May 1816. It is reported that in the first 10 days, more than 10,000 people crossed over it.

The Ha'penny Bridge is a single elliptical arch structure with a span of 42.8 metres. At the crown, it rises 3.35 metres above high water. The width is 3.6 metres. The arch rests on cantilevering granite abutments which extend 4.3 metres from the quays over the river. The original iron bridge made at Coalbrookdale in 1779 had a deck of low rise, as it had to accommodate the carriage and cart traffic of the time. The Ha'penny, by contrast, being a pedestrian bridge, could have a

larger rise, as pedestrians could ascend and descend the deck. The principal structural elements are three parallel cast iron arch ribs which span the river – one on each side and one in the centre. The ribs are formed without diagonal members and vary in their depth, (measured at 90 degrees to the intrados, i.e. the inner curve of the arch) from 1.9 metres at the springing to 0.5 metres at the crown. The ribs are made up of six segments, each about 7.2 metres long. The late Professor John W. de Courcy, in a paper, described the complex arrangement in a clear manner as follows: 'The rib sections are connected end to end with bolts and shear wedges through endplates and bearing plates. The ribs are stiffened by the deck and the diagonal and normal bracing forming a truss in the plane of the intrados. The diagonal members of this truss

are cruciform, of larger dimensions at the middle of the members than at their ends. The truss members normal to the ribs are formed from cylindrical pipe sections through which are passed round bars threaded at the ends for heavy nuts.' Diagonal cross bracing stiffens the bridge and gives lateral strength. The structure functions as an arch. The dead load (i.e. the weight of the bridge itself) plus the live load (i.e. the weight of pedestrians) causes the arch to deflect to a small degree. The arch shape distributes compression over the entire arch and transmits the weight into a horizontal thrust restrained by the abutments at either side. There is scarcely any tensile force in an arch bridge. Thus the arch shape results in compression forces along the arch. Brick and stone are strong in compression but cannot withstand much force in tension – thus these materials had historically been used for arch bridges. Cast iron in turn is ideally suited to take compression, and this is taken by the cast iron members of the arch rib of a bridge. Any tensile forces at joints are catered for by the bolts.

The concept of an arch bridge dates to the 13th century BC, where Mycenaean stone corbel-arch bridges were designed to accommodate chariots in Greece. The Romans, with their great network of roads, used arch bridges all over their empire. They understood the principles of loads and forces and had mastery of stone and brick construction. Many Roman bridges still stand today. At the same time as the Roman era, the Chinese were building advanced arch bridges.

Above

The Ha'penny Bridge leading to Bachelors Walk

Etching - 2005
5 x 27cm
Edition of 100

by **Niamh Mac Gowan**

Courtesy of the Artist

Indeed, a bridge in China still stands, dating from around AD 600, and is the world's oldest open-spandrel, stone, segmental-arch bridge. The form, span and decoration of stone arch bridges became more refined over the succeeding centuries. By the 18th century, the concept of a masonry-arch bridge was well developed in Ireland. The earliest bridges had been made of timber. Indeed the first bridge in Dublin, built by the Vikings (near the site of the present Father Mathew Bridge) at the time of the first millennium, was a simple timber structure. Timber got a new lease of life during the late 18th century in Ireland. The American engineer, Lemuel Cox, built long span road bridges of American oak in the 1790s at Wexford, Waterford, Mountgarret, Youghal and in Derry.

In 1709 Abraham Darby I rebuilt an earlier iron foundry in Coalbrook-dale by the river Severn in Shropshire. It was the ideal spot for an ironworks. There was iron ore in the neighbourhood, plus plentiful coal seams (hence the name), as well as a river to provide motive power. Steam engines were becoming more sophisticated and the Industrial Revolution was beginning to roar. The works rose to the occasion and produced cast-iron products that met the growing demand. In 1767 rudimentary cast iron rails were produced there for the mining railways, where carts of ore were pulled by horse or man.

The land owners of the district had long discussed the need for a bridge over the Severn. The existing ferry across the river was found inadequate to accommodate the growing traffic arising from the coal, iron, brick and pottery trades in the neighbourhood. When the decision was taken to build a bridge nearby over the river, what better material to use than cast-iron? The grandson of the original Darby, Abraham Darby III, produced what was the world's first iron bridge over the Severn at the eponymously named Ironbridge, not far from Coalbrookdale, in 1779. The structure, designed by Thomas Pritchard, consists of a semi-circular arch, on which sits a deck comprising two flat spans with a low rise, meeting at the crown of the bridge. At that time, there were no analytical tools to assess the forces on a bridge and thus to size the members. In this case an empirical approach was taken: the iron members, and the method of fitting together, largely mimic those of a timber truss. A conventional stone arch bridge was considered, but it was felt that construction would be slow and would disrupt the busy river traffic. The facility to join together the iron

members rapidly meant that the new bridge could be quickly built. It proved that this wonderful new material, cast iron, could be used for bridges. In the life of the great Scottish civil engineer, Thomas Telford, Samuel Smiles noting a failed attempt to build a cast iron bridge in Lyons in France, wrote that "it was reserved for English manufacturers to triumph over the difficulties that had baffled the foreign iron founders."

And so it was. Thomas Telford, as county surveyor in Shropshire built a new bridge at Buildwas, over the Severn between Shrewsbury and Bridgenorth. He had carefully examined Darby's iron bridge, but resolved to do better. The bridge consisted of a single arch of around 40 metres. It was a complex structure, with a cast iron truss arch on either side and cast iron plates forming an inner larger radius arch. There was a central deck with a low rise. *The Life of Thomas Telford* records that Telford 'had some difficulty in inducing the Coalbrookdale iron-masters, who undertook the casting of the girders, to depart from the plan

of the earlier structure.' In any case, Telford succeeded: while the new bridge was around nine metres greater in span, it used only half the weight of cast iron. Telford went on to build many road bridges in cast iron.

An unlikely early pioneer in cast iron was the philosopher and political activist Thomas Paine (who wrote the Rights of Man in 1791, which amongst other things defended the French Revolution). He had fled to America and in 1803 and presented a memoir to the American Congress on the construction of iron bridges. However, there is no record that he ever succeeded in erecting one.

Iron was first used by man around 1,200 BC, displacing the bronze of a previous age. Iron is more difficult to smelt than bronze and it took humans a long time to master the technology. Iron weapons and tools were better than bronze and this propelled the spread of the new metal. China was then the world leader in technology and it was there that cast iron was used in the 5th century BC, for weapons and agricultural tools. It took till the 15th century in Europe for cast iron to be used for artillery. By the start of the Industrial Revolution the science of preparing moulds and casting had advanced. The material has resistance to deformation and has good resistance to corrosion. Made from carbon iron alloys with a carbon content of over 2%, it tends to be brittle. It is good in compression, but poor in tension. As a result, an arch structure, such as the Ha'penny Bridge, where the main forces are compressive, suit cast iron. Furthermore, cast iron is eminently suitable for columns, where the applied vertical loads are catered for by the compressive strength of cast iron. This was a factor when the Dublin and Drogheda Railway chose to use the solid cast-iron columns, in Doric style, made in Coalbrookdale, for its new railway bridge over Sherriff Street, when the new line opened in 1844.

Above

All lined up

Detail of the bridge's railings with just two of the the many little decorative urns that break the uprights at regular intervals.

Photograph by the Author

Opposite and cover

Ha'penny Bridge

Oil on canvas - 2006
100 x 100 cm

by **Rose McGowan**

Courtesy of the Artist

Right

Stress Test

One of the many stress tests that were carried out on the bridge by Consulting Engineers, Mott MacDonald prior to its reopening to determine the bridge's loading limits.

Diagram courtesy of Mott McDonald Group Consulting Engineers

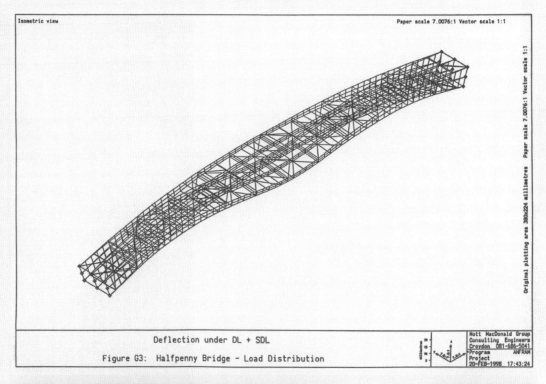

Isometric view   Paper scale 7.0076:1 Vector scale 1:1

Deflection under DL + SDL

Figure G3: Halfpenny Bridge – Load Distribution

Mott MacDonald Group
Consulting Engineers
Croydon   081-686-5041
Program   ANFRAM
Project
20-FEB-1998   17:43:24

Right

Painting with oils

With most structural work now completed on the bridge's arch, painters can now apply liberal coats of the original creamy white colour to the ironwork.

Courtesy of Dublin City Council

196

Up to the beginning of the 19th century masonry arch bridges represented the most advanced bridge building techniques in Ireland. Advances had been made in employing elliptical arches (first used in Europe, in Paris in 1775 – it was more difficult to prepare the stonework) rather than the earlier semi-circular arch shape. Thus, the construction of the Ha'penny Bridge in 1816 represented a step change – the advanced bridge technology of the time, cast iron, was introduced to Ireland from Britain, then the world leader in iron bridges. However, Dublin iron founders soon seized the initiative. The cast iron King's Bridge of 1829 was made at the nearby Phoenix ironworks at Parkgate Street. Richard Turner, ironmaster, of the Hammersmith Works in Ballsbridge, was a pioneer in cast iron and the developing new material of wrought iron. He became an expert in the design and manufacture of large span structures. One of

Left

Final resting place

The cast iron arches rest on specially carved granite ledges which form part of the abutment at the high tide mark.

Spring tides force the salt water even higher resulting in some surface rusting of the ironwork. This doesn't however affect the structural strength of the iron.

Photograph by the Author

Turner's early works was the Palm House, of 1839, in Belfast. Turner then worked on the immense structure, the Great Palm House at Kew Gardens near London, which has been described as one of the finest plant houses of the world. Now the advanced technology was moving from Dublin to the heart of empire. With Decimus Burton, Turner designed the Palm House and provided the iron sections. It was completed in 1848. Turner also built the great Curvilinear Range Building at the Botanic Gardens at Glasnevin, between 1843 and 1869. This was expertly renovated by the Office of Public Works in 1995, using similar techniques to those that were later adopted in the renovation of the Ha'penny Bridge,

Following pages

Early morning looking south

The sun illuminates the Ha'penny Bridge before the shuttered shops on Liffey Street open for business.

Photograph by the Author

INTERNET & GAMING
CENTRE

@@@@@

XBOX 360
Gaming Center

INTERNET & GAMING
CENTRE

XTREME

gorta

gorta

Heineken

Music Minds

LAVAZZA
BAKERY
AMAZINGLY
GOOD COFFEE

gorta

Mobile
Unlock &

PC & L
Rep

Console Se
YouTube

Right

An option for the bridge's entrance

Several proposals to retain the railings at the entrances were examined. These were later rejected in favour of granite stone walls designed to give pedestrians a feeling of security at the entry points.

Of interest is the original line of the steps and decking (dashed line). These were much steeper and higher at this point. The entry gradient has now been reduced in the restored structure.

The proposed lamps were never installed

Drawing courtesy of Dublin City Council

NEW STANDARD LAMPS. DESIGN CHARACTER IN SYMPATHY WITH BRIDGE

LINE OF EXISTING RAISED TIMBER DECK AND EXTENDED STONE STEPS TO BE REMOVED

NEW LIGHT WEIGHT RAMPED STEPS ALIGNED TO MATCH CAMBER OF ARCH

NEW RAILINGS TO MATCH EXISTING AT ABUTMENT PERIMETER ONLY

NEW CUT STONE PIER AND CAPPING

EXISTING TOLL HOUSE PLATFORMS REMOVED

PEDESTRIAN RESEVOIR

EXISTING COPING STONE TO ABUTMENTS FORMING PARAPET WALL TO PEDESTRIAN RESEVOIR

NEW GRANITE STEPS

SECTION: OPTION 2   scale: 1:50

Drawing No. 347/04

Right

Aerial view

The bridge from the air with Lower Ormond Quay on the left and Wellington Quay on the right.

Courtesy of Dublin City Council

an equally successful project. Other large and successful Dublin iron founders were Mallets and Courtney, Stephens & Bailey. These profited from the railway boom, building railway equipment as well as railway bridges made of the advanced material of the time, wrought iron – cast iron for bridges was in course of being eclipsed. Developments such as the Bessemer smelting process meant that steel became widely available towards the end of the 19th century. At that time the Irish ironworks were eclipsed when it came to large span steel bridges: the Loop line Railway Bridge in Dublin of 1891 was made by William Arrol of Glasgow. They also supplied the Barrow Bridge of 1906, close to Waterford City. At 650 metres, it is still the longest railway bridge in the Republic of Ireland.

The Ha'penny Bridge has served Dublin well over the years. However by the end of its second century, this cast-iron structure was in need of rehabilitation. In 1998 Dublin Corporation commissioned an assessment of the bridge. Many options were considered, ranging from merely preserving it as an ornamental structure, to a thorough structural rehabilitation so that it could continue as a working bridge. The latter option was chosen and the bridge was closed for works in early 2001. A temporary Bailey bridge was erected adjacent to the bridge, to allow pedestrians access across the river while the work was going on. The railings were disassembled for repair and restoration off site, eight plan bracing members that connected the main arch ribs that had failed were replaced to match existing members. Repairs were carried out to any cracks in the main arch ribs using the *Metalock Process* and the entire bridge (arch ribs, deck and railings) were blast cleaned and painted and all joints sealed to deal with corrosion. Over 1,000 individual pieces of railings were carefully removed and sent for repair and restoration. On close examination

Above

Merchant's Arch from the Ha'penny Bridge
*Pencil Drawing
Size 22 x 24cm*
by Desmond McCarthy
Courtesy of the Artist

Right

It's not art

This is actually a cross section of a piece of flaking paint taken from the bridge before restoration. Viewed in an electron microscope it reveals the several original layers of creamy white paint at the bottom. This was then followed by layers of black and silver paint.

Centre right

Railing upright detail

Every facet of the bridge was examined in the utmost detail in order to make sure that all restoration work was carried out as faithfully to the original designs of the bridge as possible.

This drawing shows the typical attention to detail of just one of the railings uprights of the bridge.

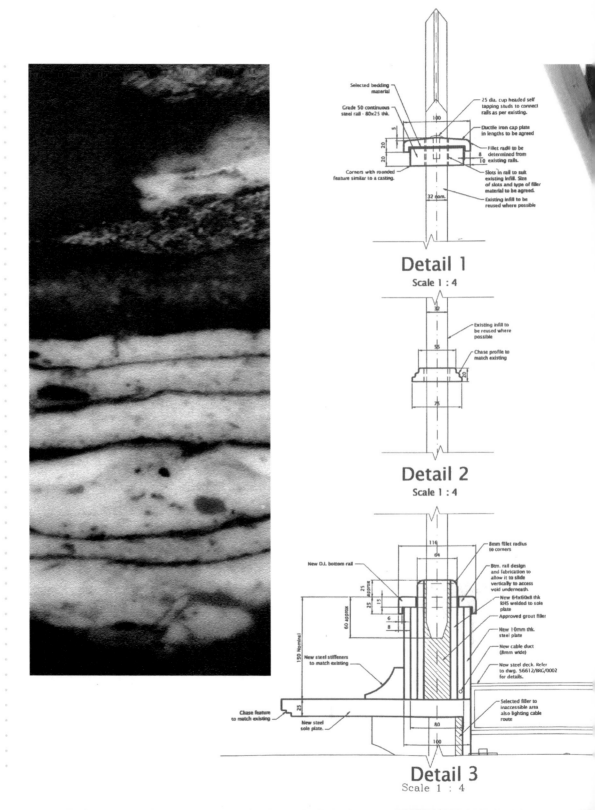

Detail 1
Scale 1 : 4

Selected bedding material

Grade 50 continuous steel rail - 80x25 thk.

Corners with rounded feature similar to a casting.

25 dia. cup headed self tapping studs to connect rails as per existing.

Ductile iron cap plate in lengths to be agreed

Fillet radii to be determined from existing rails.

Slots in rail to suit existing infill. Size of slots and type of filler material to be agreed.

Existing infill to be reused where possible

Detail 2
Scale 1 : 4

Existing infill to be reused where possible

Chase profile to match existing

Detail 3
Scale 1 : 4

New D.I. bottom rail

New steel stiffeners to match existing

Chase feature to match existing

New steel sole plate.

8mm fillet radius to corners

Btm. rail design and fabrication to allow it to slide vertically to access void underneath.

New 64x60x8 thk RHS welded to sole plate

Approved grout filler

New 10mm thk. steel plate

New cable duct (8mm wide)

New steel deck. Refer to dwg. S6612/BRG/0002 for details.

Selected filler to inaccessible area also lighting cable route

Above left

Under the bridge

This is the view few of us see. Of interest is the build up of dirt particles that invisibly sweep around the river and adhere to the underside of the bridge where the rain can't wash it off.

Also of note is that the bridge not only carries pedestrians but also essential services such as telecoms and electrical cables in aluminium ducts from one side of the river to the other.

Lights that illuminate the bridge at night are also housed discreetly out of sight.

Photographs and drawings courtesy of Dublin City Council

Above

The Ha'penny Bridge

Ink and Bleach - 2011
Size 15 x 21cm

by **Liing Heaney**

Courtesy of the Artist

the elements of the superstructure were found to be generally sound apart from cracking generated by the expansive forces caused by corrosion in the many joints. The policy was to retain as large a portion of the original members as possible. Of the original ironwork approximately 98% was reused. For those pieces which were replicated, care was taken to reproduce the slightly worn and pitted surface that was characteristic of old cast iron in similar structures. A new bridge deck in steel was installed and this was covered by a slip-resistant aggregate finish. Safer pedestrian entrance and exit points were provided at each side by widening, curving and smoothing the bridge mouths. The structural work being completed, the bridge was painted in the original off-white colour. It reopened on 21 December 2001.

The outstanding attention to detail and the successful rehabilitation was recognised when the reconstruction was recognised by a European Union Cultural Heritage/Europe Nostra Award, Europe's most prestigious heritage prize in 2002.

Of special merit were the following individuals and companies who took part in the restoration and included; Michael Phillips, City Engineer, Dublin City Council; Mott McDonald EPO Ltd, Consulting Engineers; Paul Arnold, Conservation Architect; Patrick Gorman, Senior Executive Engineer and overall project manager for Dublin City Council. Enterprise Ireland provided specialist advice in relation to cleaning and painting cast iron work, Irishenco Construction Ltd were the main contractors. Harland and Wolff of Belfast were appointed as sub-contractors for all metal and railing restoration works and Gabriel Hughes Contracts Ltd supervised blast cleaning and painting works.

The 200th anniversary of the Ha'penny Bridge was celebrated on 19 May 2016. It has served the people of Dublin well for two centuries and, given the care and attention it has received, it should continue to do so well into its third century.

Left

The Lamp Standards

One of the three lamp standards that grace the bridge. These and the other two help support and brace the railings of the bridge.

Below left

Job well done

This bronze plaque mounted at the bridge's northern entrance records the individuals, companies and civic bodies who helped with the bridge's restoration and reconstruction,

Photographs by the Author

Following pages

The bridge revealed

The view from the Winding Stair restaurant on Lower Ormond Quay reveals the elegant lines of a structure that will never date.

Photograph by the Author

Perversion at the Winding Stair Bookshop & Café

by Alan Jude Moore

Three floors above the Ha'penny Bridge
The wind off the Liffey howling like a new religion
through the streets
A prophet in a raincoat holds court in Russian
A jazz guitar tunes every napkin to poetry
The Dutch tourist keeps time with his pen on the ashtray
A French girl might be sketching me
I do my best to look across the room capable of something

I realise I have no favourite woman and no mother tongue

Speaking the language of short affairs and civic buildings
Proposed afternoons Che Guevara credit cards

I miss the alcoholics
The five in the morning bulls hit
Thinking now of a woman's dry oligarchy
The order of her heart
The meritocracy of her sex

'Perversion at the Winding Stair Bookshop & Café'
from *Black State Cars* (Salmon Poetry, 2004).
Reproduced with the permission of the publisher.

Marking the
Millennium

A tale of
two bridges

7

A tale of
two bridges

by Seán Harrington

Principal, Seán Harrington Architects, Dublin

Preceding pages
The River Liffey

The Millennium Bridge traverses the river, complementing its near neighbour.

While both bridges perform the same task, nearly 200 years of bridge building design and technology separate their fabrication.

Opposite
The southern entrance to the bridge

Photographs by the Author

o design happens in isolation. It is always influenced by what has gone before.

When we designed the Millennium Bridge in 1998, our foremost intention was to design a bridge that sat comfortably in its historic and urban context – in time and place.

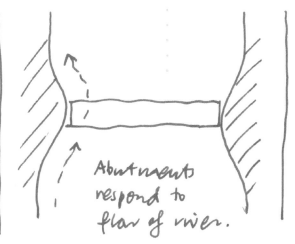

Above
Responding to the flow of the river

An architect's sketch of the layout of the abutments and their relation with the river

Drawing courtesy of Howley, Harrington Architects

The River Liffey in the city centre is arguably Dublin's greatest public space. It is defined by the almost continuous terrace walls of four and five storey buildings along the quays. The river is sufficiently wide to give clear distinction between north and south, yet narrow enough to be able to look across and recognise a face. It's both of a city and human scale.

Between Ormond and Wellington Quays the river is about 55 metres wide, flows eastwards towards Dublin Bay, and is tidal with a range of about 4 metres between the lowest and highest water marks. The fluvial stream is contained by great granite quay walls topped with elegant rounded stone parapets. The dominant object in this stretch of the river is the Ha'penny Bridge. Given its great cultural, artistic and social significance we were inspired to design the new bridge to sit comfortably and be 'in polite conversation' with its older relative, yet have a confident, contemporary and appropriate expression of its own.

The question was; how could we achieve this?

The Ha'penny Bridge is a beautiful iconic design that has become an instantly recognisable symbol of Dublin. It is a bridge built using the most advanced technology of its day, crossing the river with a single elegant span that jumps off one stone abutment and lands on another. It theatrically arches across the river, allowing boats to pass beneath and people to walk up and over.

Structurally, it is an arch made of cast iron with the depth of the truss decreasing towards the middle of the span, elegantly thinning out in the centre of the river. This makes it look daring; almost reaching towards the sky, then holding its breath, before gently landing on the opposite quayside. All structure is below the walking-deck. The apparent simplicity of the design is achieved using a limited pallet of materials: masonry for the abutments and cast-iron for the arched truss and balustrading. This visually articulates and differentiates the abutments, rooted in the land, from the arched truss, flying through the air.

For the Millennium Bridge, our initial design decision was also to have a single span bridge, with the structure below deck. This simple move would start the aesthetic conversation between Ha'penny and Millennium bridges, and would avoid extravagant and unnecessary structural gestures like masts, cables or above-deck arches that would distract from its illustrious neighbour.

Having decided on this basic principle, our next aim was efficiency in engineering. This invariably ensures the most visually elegant solution, uses the least amount of material and is often the most cost effective. In our case, engineering excellence was provided by Price and Myers, who determined that a shallow arched truss was the most efficient solution. The challenge was then to find a way in which this could be achieved with the deck being as flat as possible. This was important to ensure that, unlike the Ha'penny Bridge, wheelchairs, children's buggies and bicycles could get from one side to the other without having to go up steps.

Below

The Millennium Bridge

Photograph - 2001

An interesting view of the recently completed bridge showing heavy commercial traffic on the quays which has now abated due to use of the Port Tunnel. The Liffey Boardwalk has yet to be constructed.

Images courtesy of Howley, Harrington Architects

The Ha'penny Bridge achieved the single span by having a relatively tall arch. This is an efficient structural shape that resolves the structural forces down to the abutments in a reasonable way, by reducing the horizontal element of the load. The down side is that this tall arch needs steps (or originally, a very steep ramp) for pedestrians to get over it. As an arch flattens, which would have to be the case with the Millennium Bridge, it is a much greater technological challenge to span this distance,

Submission Elevation Drawing of the Millennium Bridge

Note: Wellington Quay, is 1.5m higher than Lower Ormond Quay.

Key to Elevation

1 Wellington Quay

2 Stoneclad Spreadwaters

3 Abutment Railings

4 Lighting Columns

5 Arched Truss

6 Leaning Rails and Balusters

7 Aluminium Deck

8 Cast Stone Bollard

whilst still keeping the truss shallow to allow navigable headroom beneath, and for visual elegance.

Simply put, as the arch flattens, the proportion of horizontal load at the ends increases. To absorb these huge forces, one way would have been to install massive concrete piled foundations behind the quay walls under the quayside roads. However, this would have meant closing the quays to traffic for months, and as they are the primary transport route to and from the city centre, was impossible. It would also have caused significant and irreparable damage to the historic quay walls - something we were keen to avoid if possible.

Working with the engineers, it was instead decided that these large horizontal loads would be transferred to the bedrock using portal frame technology, resolving all the structural forces on the river side of the quay walls, thereby avoiding the need for foundations under the quay roads. This was achieved using very large concrete triangular, pivoting haunches, supported off foundations in the river, to which the steel truss would be fixed.

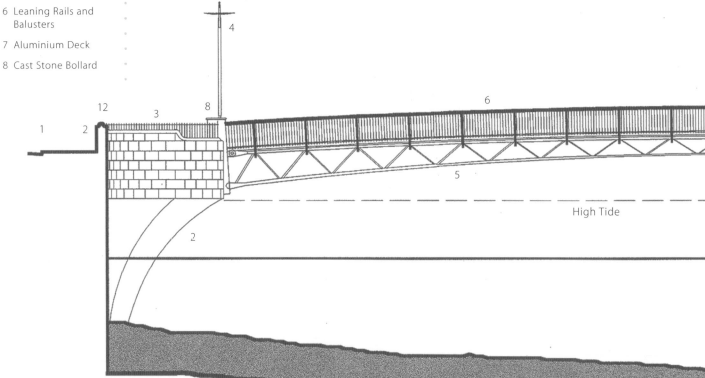

Normally, foundations in the river are constructed using cofferdams – temporary waterproof enclosures usually made of steel sheet piling. This is expensive, time consuming to install and prone to leaks, which causes delays in the construction process. Given the immovable Millennium deadline and the tight budget, we wanted to try and avoid the use of cofferdams. From our own historical research into the construction of both Grattan and Ha'penny bridges we knew that the bedrock at the bottom of the river was relatively high. This was confirmed by looking at the river at low tide when you could see the bedrock exposed to view. This gave us the idea that the foundations could be designed so that the contractor could cast the foundations during low tides, working in the dry, without using cofferdams.

Having established the foundation design, and with the haunches for the portal frame positioned on the outside of the quay walls, we then gave careful consideration to the design of the abutments themselves.

Below

Elevation of the Millennium Bridge

Architect's preliminary drawing of the bridge, showing the steel truss, concrete abutments and the other elements required for the bridge.

Drawing courtesy of Howley, Harrington Architects

Key to Elevation

9 Precast Concrete Fin
10 Access void to Spot Lights
11 Aerated Concrete Fill
12 Quay Walls
13 Pad Foundations
14 Rock Anchors for foundations
15 Rock Anchors for concrete shell
16 Lower Ormond Quay

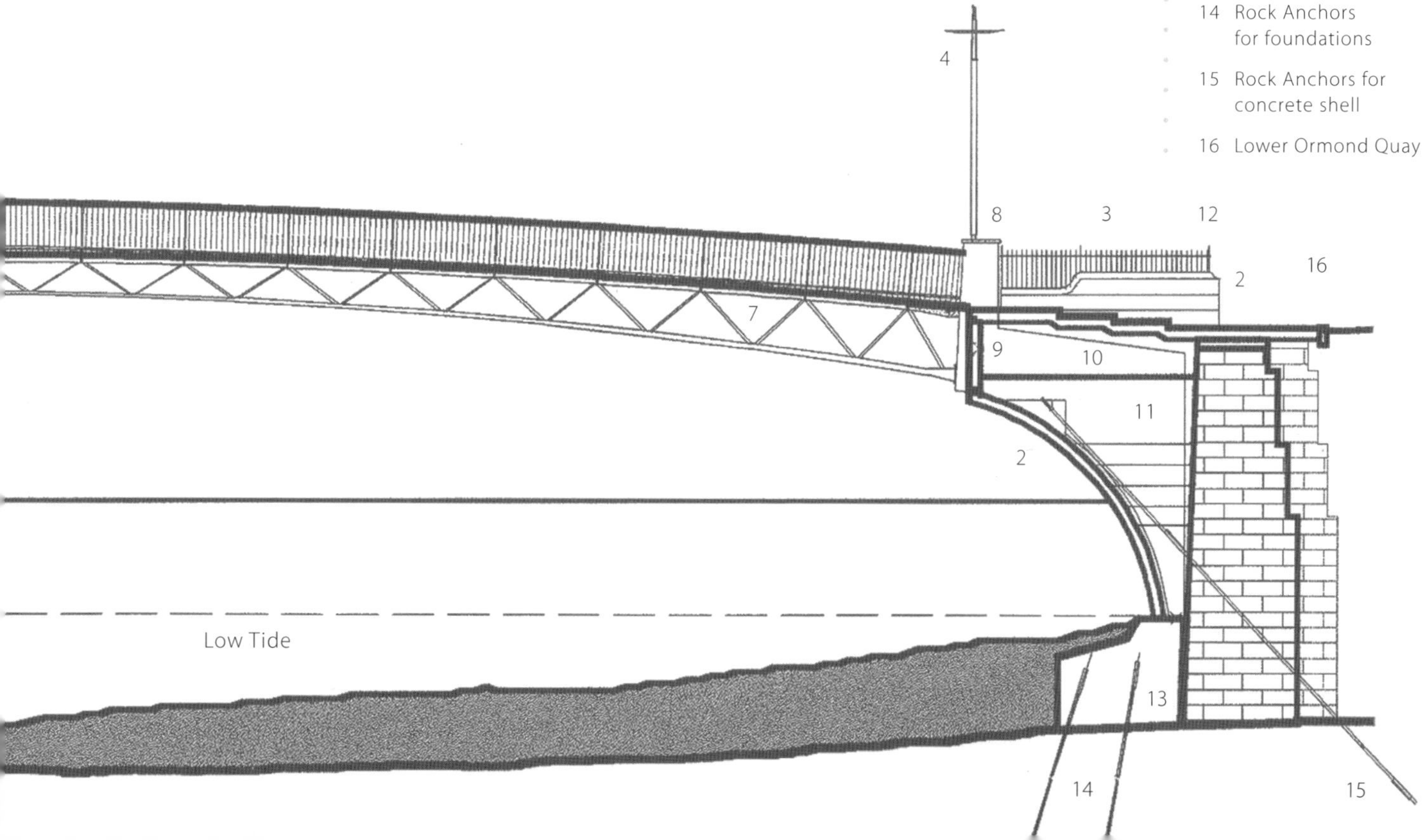

Right

Millennium abutment; where stone and steel meet

The white granite stonework has now weathered to an even shade of grey and blends into the quay walls on both sides of the river.

Photograph by the Author

Opposite

Lifting Dublin's Millennium Bridge into place

Oil on canvas - 1999 Size 27 x 33cm

by **Peter Pearson**

Courtesy of the Artist

On Sunday 7 November 1999 the completed truss is lowered into position.

It had earlier been transported from Carlow, where it was fabricated, some 90 kms south-west of Dublin in one piece.

Firstly we reminded ourselves of the arrangement at the Ha'penny Bridge. Here, the abutments are also on the river side of the quay walls. These are made of stone but constructionally and visually distinct from the quay walls, butting up against them. They project perpendicularly from the face of the quay walls, before turning the corner with a concave curve to reach the outer face, parallel to the river, which receives the end of the truss.

The concrete structural haunches at either end of the Millennium Bridge are also at right angles to the quay walls. However, we decided to encase them with curved concrete shells, forming spreadwaters so that the river or tidal forces could gently flow around the abutments in either direction at any tidal condition, thereby reducing the fluvial force on them. Low down near the foundations this curve has a small diameter, and as it rises, the spread water gets wider and deeper to encase the haunches, echoing a wineglass shape.

At the top, the shape of the widest part of the spread-water then defined the shape and extent of the pavement on the abutment. This provided a really useful place where people could stand before crossing the road, in contrast to the arrangement at the Ha'penny Bridge, where the narrow footpath at the bottom of the steps gets congested where people wait for the red light to turn green. Instead, we created small public places; wide extensions of the footpath and a definite threshold to the bridge.

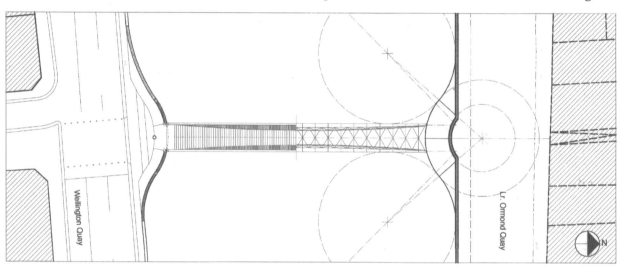

The lower parts of the spread water shells (that were in the tidal river zone) were left as fair-faced concrete, as soon this would be covered by green algae and river deposits. Above this, the vertical surfaces of the spread waters were clad with recycled stone taken from the demolition of the original balustrade walling. The visual effect of this was to make the spreadwater shells look like a natural bellying out of the quay walls, thereby seamlessly integrating the abutments into the quay wall, in contrast to the arrangement at the Ha'penny Bridge.

The surface of the abutments was paved in granite similar to the quayside pavements, as a natural extension of them. At the threshold between the abutment and bridge the walking surface changes to aluminium plank flooring, to reinforce the distinction between lightweight metal bridge and heavy stone abutments, like the Ha'penny Bridge. Unlike the Ha'penny Bridge, the threshold is level, so that the Millennium Bridge can be crossed without going up any steps or steep slopes.

Right

The structure of the Millennium Bridge

While the bridge is carried on a lightweight truss it was designed to look strong and reassure the pedestrians crossing. Two shoulder height entry towers reinforce this along with a wide handrail and a solid aluminium deck.

The bridge is bounded by two major traffic arteries along the quays. Adequate provision had to be made for the expected throng of pedestrians, waiting here before crossing.

Photograph by the Author

Key to Railings

1 Aluminium - Bronze Leaning Rail

2 Fibreoptic Harnesses

3 Lighting Lens

4 Stainless Steel Cover Plate

5 Stainless Steel Elliptical Section with Vertical Balustrades

6 Painted Steel Upright

7 Stainless Steel Kickrail

8 Duplex Cast Steel Outrigger

9 Mill finished Aluminium Deck

10 Painted Steel Channel Section

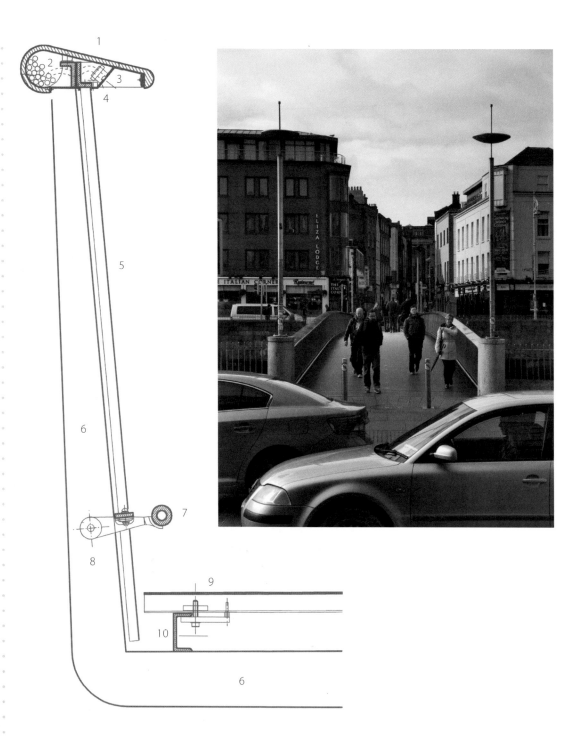

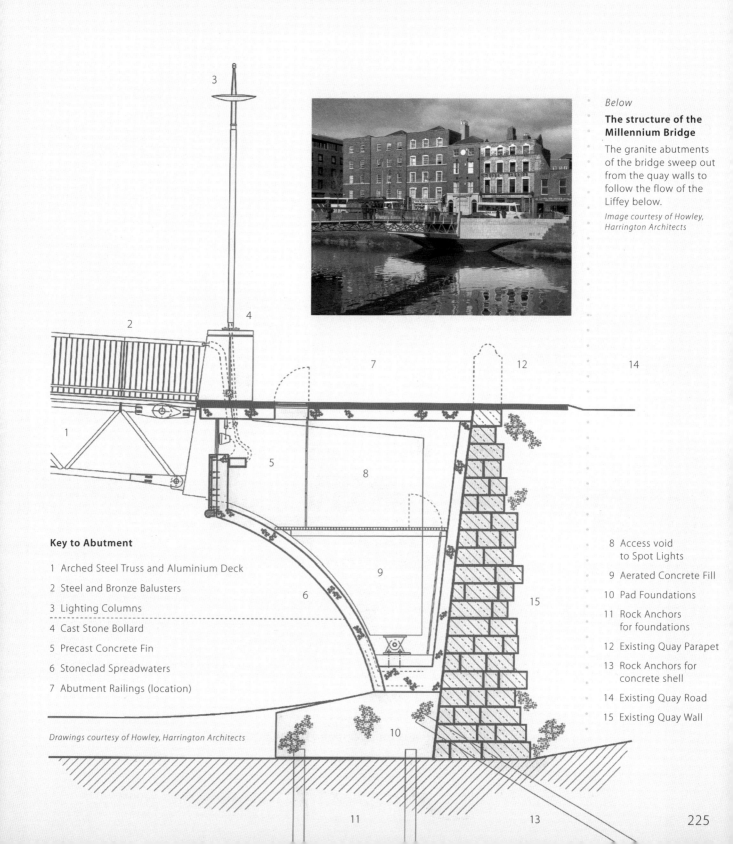

Key to Abutment

1 Arched Steel Truss and Aluminium Deck

2 Steel and Bronze Balusters

3 Lighting Columns

4 Cast Stone Bollard

5 Precast Concrete Fin

6 Stoneclad Spreadwaters

7 Abutment Railings (location)

8 Access void to Spot Lights

9 Aerated Concrete Fill

10 Pad Foundations

11 Rock Anchors for foundations

12 Existing Quay Parapet

13 Rock Anchors for concrete shell

14 Existing Quay Road

15 Existing Quay Wall

Drawings courtesy of Howley, Harrington Architects

225

Above
Liffey Bridges
Oil on canvas - 2010
Size 25 x 33cm
by **Liam Daly**
Courtesy of the Artist

When designing the balustrading for the Millennium Bridge we also looked to the Ha'penny Bridge for inspiration, and to see what could be improved. Interestingly, the balustrading for the Ha'penny Bridge is the same material as its arched truss. This simplicity works well. However, the sharp-pointed balustrade posts are up to shoulder height, presumably to give a feeling of safety for the users, but this results in a feeling of excessive enclosure.

Nowhere on the Ha'penny Bridge are you specifically encouraged to stop and look at the river - it's a bridge to get from one side to the other in an efficient way. In contrast, we wanted the Millennium Bridge to be a place to linger. For this reason we decided to keep the balustrading to the minimum permissible safe height above the deck level and instead of topping it with either sharp railings or a handrail (which is really unnecessary on a flat bridge), we decided to use an aluminium-bronze leaning rail, a wide angled surface you could lean on with your elbows and enjoy the view of the river and the Ha'penny Bridge. Similarly to the Ha'penny Bridge we used vertical balustrade bars. However in our case instead of fat square sections, we chose stainless steel elliptical bars. Seen from a distance, side on, they look thin (adding to the sense of transparency for the bridge) and when seen walking across the bridge they look fatter and give a secure sense of enclosure.

Lighting for the Ha'penny Bridge is a very elegant solution. Above head height there are three lanterns on decorative brackets that span across the bridge from one balustrade to the other, and as a pedestrian you pass under these archways when crossing the bridge. These brackets also give the balustrade panels some lateral support, by connecting each side together. The lanterns give good overhead light for facial recognition and are a beautiful design feature.

Consistent with the overall design principles, we wanted to avoid any overhead structure whatsoever on the Millennium Bridge truss and so decided to locate the deck lighting underneath the handrail, hidden, and shining downwards. These are supplemented by uplighters within the deck, like landing lights running along the centre of the bridge.

All lighting used fibre optics, which was the latest technology at the time of designing. This has been the least successful part of the design of the Millennium Bridge, giving a dull level of light all the way across the bridge, most of the time. Designing today we certainly would have used LED lights, which are long-lasting, energy-efficient, small and easily concealed.

So in many ways the design of the Millennium Bridge was inspired by the Ha'penny Bridge, encouraging us to design a bridge that was low-key and respectful to its setting, and in its form, sharing some design features, interpreted in a contemporary way. Similarities include a below-deck metal arched truss structural solution, with metal balustrading, and masonry abutments. On matters of detail we also

looked to see what worked and didn't work so well and took inspiration accordingly.

The result is a new bridge that sits comfortably next to its older sister, and has become in the best sense, a seamless and accepted piece of civic infrastructure for citizens to use and enjoy.

Like the Ha'penny Bridge, the Millennium Bridge is an example of how a bridge can harness the best technology of its day without being overly designed or contorted for the sake of appearances or novelty. This indicates a good marriage between architecture and engineering, and is fundamental to good design that will never go out of fashion.

Every design is influenced by what went before, and the Millennium Bridge itself became an important inspiration for the next bridge in Dublin that I had the privilege of being the architect for – the Rosie Hackett Bridge, completed in 2015. Here, working with engineers Roughan and O'Donovan, we also wanted to design a bridge that was low-key and respectful to the setting next to O'Connell Bridge. In the same way as the Millennium Bridge, it is a single span bridge, using the portal frame below-deck structural principle, with curved abutments on the riverside of the quay walls, only this time made of concrete to take the weight of the LUAS and buses. Similarly we celebrated the threshold between abutment and bridge with tall portal lights, this time doubling up as the structural columns to support the overhead LUAS cabling.

Opposite
The Millennium Bridge
Oil on canvas - 1999
Size 25 x 33cm
by **Peter Pearson**
Courtesy of the Artist

As an architect I am continually inspired by William Morris's golden rule, to 'Have nothing... that you do not know to be useful, or believe to be beautiful.'

The Ha'penny Bridge is as useful and beautiful today as it was the day it was built. It has inspired the design of the Millennium Bridge, which in turn was an influence for the Rosie Hackett Bridge; a baton of influence being passed down through the years, flowing with the river, unique to Dublin.

Sean Harrington was Partner in Charge and Project Architect for the Millennium Bridge, Howley Harrington Architects.

Above
Rosie Hackett Bridge
The main objective for the new bridge was to convey the latest LUAS tram line and other bus services over the Liffey at this point. However its secondary role also provides a much needed open space with seating where Dubliners can relax and enjoy the ambiance of the city in a riverside setting.
Photograph by the Author

Liffey Swim

by Jessica Traynor

In the dream, the Blessington Street Basin
fills with the Liffey's stout-bottle waters,
but still the swimmers come, in droves,
on the stray sovereign of an Irish summer's day.

The river courses through the city,
turning concrete roadways to canal banks
that shrug their shoulders into dark water,
a man rises, seal-like in his caul of silt, to wave.

At the sluice gate, where the river bends
out of sight between toppling buildings,
a black dog jumps, again and again into water.

And there, at the edge of vision, my parents,
ready to join the swimmers,
gester their cheerful farewells.

Night *into* day

into night

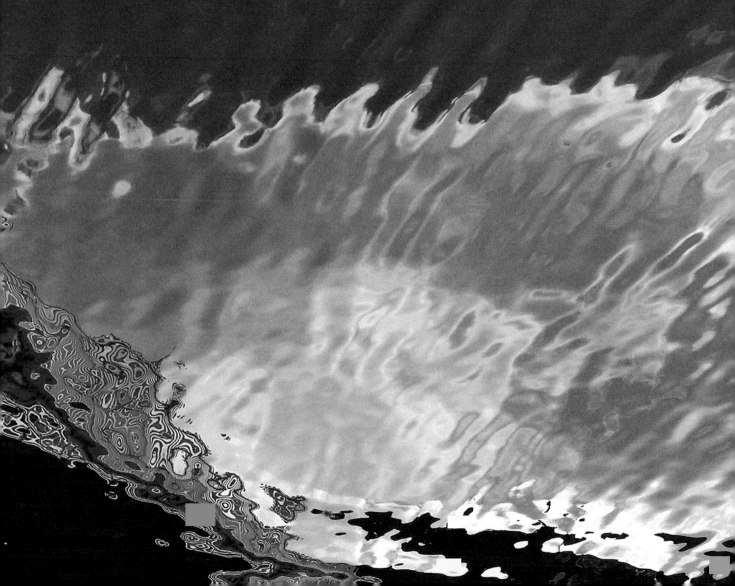

Capturing tidal and climatic variations

00·09

Friday 29 April

04·30

Friday 24 June

05·10

Thursday 5 May

05·41

Monday 18 April

06·39

Tuesday 27 March

Monday 9 May

07·30

Tuesday 27 March

07·44

Thursday 9 August

08·34

Monday 26 March

09·49

Sunday 8 May

13·51

Tuesday 19 April

15:24

Monday 9 May

249

16·34

Wednesday 8 June

17·16

Tuesday 19 April

18·15

Thursday 5 May

19·11

Tuesday   26 March

20·02

Monday 26 March

21·58

Monday 13 June

In the City

by Rhoda Coghill

Gently in the night flows my river, the Liffey.
It is mine by right of love, this river always
Running, since childhood, under my feet, always
Branching along my veins - this river of birds,
Avenue of serene, Ascendancy swans,
Trail of the single gunman cormorant,
Stage of the seagulls' ballet - those faery visitors
Who cry and perch and fly, blown in the air
Like paper toys.
                         Tonight there are no birds;
The thickening mist blinds me to all but light.
By day small painted boats, wings
Of coloured parrots, tighten their holding ropes
And lie beside the wall. Pale women
Hurry across the bridges, dawdle at windows,
Treasure their handbags, intend on finding bargains.
Crowds at the rush-hour of a Spring afternoon
Move in the clean patterns of thrown confetti.
                         But now
In fog the city covers all its candour.
From windowed vehicles the light
Imprints a moving tartan on the water;
And where a street-lamp hangs a luminous triangle,
There, mirrored, a three-sided corresponding
Euclidean figure breaks the river's blackness,
Base to base applied, with lamp-post perpendicular
And tree subtending.
                Now
Where are the seabirds? Do they fly
At day's end to the sea, to spend the night
One-legged on rock, in thought?
When, rarely, moves a patch
Offaint illumination on the darkest water,
Then are discovered small waiting forms,
Patiently floating, homeless, through the dark
They do not understand. Silence
Holds them, until daylight.

Acknowledgments

The Author would particulary like to thank the following authors who kindly contributed chapters for the book.

Michael B. Barry

Annette Black

David de Haan

Seán Harrington

Michael Phillips

Logan Sisley

Gerard Smyth

I would also like to thank Michael Phillips, Former City Engineer, Dublin City Council for arranging funding for this book.

Also Dr Mary Clark, Dublin City Archivist who along with her staff at the Dublin City Library and Archives gave unstinting support for the project.

I would also like to thank Eibhlin Colgan, Archive Manager, Guinness Archives, Diagio plc who assisted the author with the Guinness chapter.

A special thanks to the following individuals and organisations who supplied artifacts, material, histories, artwork and other information.

Without their help this book would not have been possible.

Alljoy Design

An Post & General Post Office

Paul Arnold Architects

Brian Ballard

John D Benson

Smiley Bolger

Pat Boran

Emily Boylan

Robbie Bray

Tom Byrne

Carrolls Irish Gifts

Rhoda Coghill

The Colley Family

Declan Collinge

Dedalus Press

Dublin City Council

Dublin City Gallery The Hugh Lane

Liam Daly

David Farren

Flyleaf Press

Patrick Gorman, Senior Executive Engineer Dublin City Council

Paul Goulding

Mary Grey

Kevin Griffin

Guinness Archives

Jenny Gunning

John Hallett

James Hardiman Library, National University of Ireland Galway

Sean Harrington Architects

Sean Hillen

Howley, Harrington Architects

Siobhan Hyde

Ironbridge Gorge Museum Trust, Shropshire

Peadar Kearney

Maureen Kennelly

The Liberties Association

Liffey Players, Alberta, Canada

Liing Heaney

Daniel Lipstein

Desmond McCarthy

Grainne McDermott, Executive Engineer Dublin City Council

Dara MacDonaill, Irish Times

Niamh MacGowan

Rose McGowan

Donal MacPolin

Francis Matthews

Allan Jude Moore

Robert Morrissey

Mott McDonald Group Consulting Engineers

Mullingar Pewter

National Library of Ireland

O'Brien Press

Liam O'Broin

Helen O'Carroll

Niall O'Connor

Perry Ogden

Peter Pearson

David Penney

Poetry Ireland

Premier Dairies

Robin-Ruth UK Ltd

Simon Roche

Sarah Rogers

Jim Ryan

Tony Schorman, Lír Coins & Collectables

Science Museum, London

Kevin Shortis

Michael Skelton

Joanne Smith

Juan Bosco Somonos

Martin Stone

Jessica Traynor

Richard Walshe Workhouse Visual Communications

Kasper Zier

Bibliography

Barry, Michael - Across Deep Waters, Bridges of Ireland, Frankfort Press, 1985

Bennet, Douglas - The Encyclopedia of Dublin, Gill & Macmillan, 2005

Black, Annette; Barry, Michael - Bridges of Dublin, the Remarkable Story of Dublin's Liffey Bridges, Dublin City Council, 2015

Bourke, Edward - The Guinness Story: The Family, The Business, The Black Stuff O'Brien Press, 2009

Corcoran, Tony - The Goodness of Guinness: The Brewery, Its People and the City of Dublin. Liberties Press, 2005

Cox, Ronald; Gould, Michael - Ireland's Bridges, Wolfhound Press, 2003

Dawson, Barbara - Hugh Lane and the Origins of the Collection, in Images and Insights, Hugh Lane Municipal Gallery of Modern Art, Dublin, 1993

de Courcey, John W. - The Liffey in Dublin, Gill and Macmillan, 1996

de Courcey, John - The Ha'penny Bridge in Dublin, Journal of the Institution of Structural Engineers, Vol 69, No. 3, February, 1991

de Haan, David - Coalbrookdale and the Iron Bridge in The International Journal for the History of Engineering & Technology, Vol 85, No 2. Newcomen Society, 2015

Dennison S.R; MacDonagh O. - Guinness 1886 – 1939: From Incorporation to the Second World War. Cork University Press, 1998

Davies, J - The Book of Guinness Advertising. Guinness Publishing Ltd, 1998

Dublin Divided - Exhibition catalogue, Dublin City Gallery The Hugh Lane, Dublin, 2013

Freeman's Journal Archives, The

Gilbert, John Thomas - Calendar of Ancient Records of Dublin in the Possession of the Municipal Corporation of that City, Ulan Press, 2012

Guinness, P - Arthur's Round: The Life and Times of Brewing Legend Arthur Guinness. Peter Owen, 2008

Herrero, Marta - Irish Intellectuals and Aesthetics: The Making of a Modern Art Collection, Irish Academic Press, Dublin, 2007

Hughes, David - 'A Bottle of Guinness Please' The Colourful History of Guinness. Phimboy Publishing, 2006

Hugh Lane: Founder of a Gallery of Modern Art for Ireland, Scala, London, 2008

Irish Times Archives, The

Klingender, Francis (ed Arthur Elton) - The Art of the Industrial Revolution. Paladin, 1968

Liberties Association, The - The Liffey Bridges Project Typescript, 1987

Mallagh, Joseph - City Bridges over the Liffey, present and future, IEI Transactions, Vol 65, 1939

McDiarmid, Lucy - Hugh Lane and the Decoration of Dublin, in The Irish Art of Controversy, Lilliput Press, Dublin, 2005

Mullally, F - The Silver Salver: The Story of the Guinness Family. Granada, 1980

O'Keefe, Peter - Irish Stone Bridges, Irish Academic Press, 1991

Phillips, Michael; Hamilton, Albert - Project History of Dublin's River Liffey Bridges, Proc. ICE, London, BE 156, 2003

Revolutionary States: Home Rule and Modern Ireland, Exhibition catalogue, Dublin City Gallery The Hugh Lane, Dublin, 2012

Rice, Peter - An Engineer Imagines. Artemis, 1994

Rynne, Colin - Industrial Ireland 1750 -1930, Collins Press, 2006

Semple, George - A Treatise on Building in Water in Two Parts, Gale ECCO, Print Editions, 2010

Sharp, Neil - The wrong Twigs for an Eagle's Nest? Architecture, Nationalism and Sir Hugh Lane's Scheme for a Gallery of Modern Art, 1904-13, in The Architecture of the Museum:

Symbolic Structures, Urban Contexts, Manchester University Press, Manchester, 2003

Skempton, A. W., ed. - Biographical Dictionary of Civil Engineers, Volume 1, 1500 - 1830. Thomas Telford, London, 2002

Smiles, Samuel, - The Life of Thomas Telford; 1867, Cambridge Library Collection.

Thomas, Emyr - Coalbrookdale and the Darbys. Sessions Book Trust in association with the Ironbridge Gorge Museum Trust, 1999

Trinder, Barrie - The Industrial Archaeology of Shropshire. Phillimore, 1996

Tutty, M.J - Bridges over the Liffey, Dublin Historical Record, Vol XXXV, 1981

Yenne, Bill - Guinness: The 250 Year Quest for the Perfect Pint. Wiley Publications, 2007

Vialls, Christine - Coalbrookdale and the Iron Revolution, Cambridge University Press, 1980

Index

Abbey Theatre - 95
Abercynon - 49
Abutment - 187, 190, 219, 220, 222, 229, 231
Abutment plan - 213
Act of Union - 156
Advertising - 71
Alljoy Design - 171
Alpine Tunnelling Method - 133
American Congress - 195
An Post, Irish Stamp - 77
Ardilaun, Lord - 89
'A Treatise on Building in Water' - 184
Aston Quay - 102/103
Austin 7 'Baby' car - 73/74
Austin 7 'Baby' - 72/73
Armstrong, Walter - 90
Arnold, Paul - 183, 185, 186
Arnold, Paul (Architect) - 205
Arrol, William - 201
Art Gallery Site - Another Suggestion - 109

Bacon, Francis Artist's Studio - 92/93
Bagnio Slip - 23, 63
'Bailey' Bridge - 201
Ballard, Brian - 14/15, 87
Ballsbridge - 197
Barkley, W.M (Ship) - 139
Barrack Bridge - 155
Barrow Bridge, Waterford - 201
Bedlam Furnace - 41
Belfast - 138
Benson, John D - 74
Beresford, John Claudius - 63, 64, 67, 71, 156
Bernard Shaw, George - 100, 101, 166, 169
Bessemer Process - 201
Birds View of Dublin 1889 - 26/27
Birmingham - 33, 45
Black Country - 46
Blast Furnace, 18th century - 47
Bloom, Leopold - 158
Bodkin, Dr. Thomas - 91, 109, 111
Bolger, Similey - 166
Borough Surveyor - 75
Booth, Mr. - 169
Boran, Pat - 179
Botanic Gardens, Dublin - 197

Boylan Emily - 130
Brady, Robbie - 166
Brownrigg Craig, Francis - 95
Brewster, Gordon - 104
Brewster, Gordon - 109
Brewer, H W - 26/27
Britain - 123, 135, 139, 144
Brocas, Samuel Frederick - 58/59
Bridewell, The - 155
Bridge Crib or Support - 61
Bridges of Dublin', Book - 25
Bristol Channel - 186
British Empire - 156
British Army - 138, 158
Buildwas Bridge - 45, 192
Burkes Shop - 162
Burton, Decimus - 197
Byrne, Tom - 24

Canterbury & Whitstable Railway - 53
Capel Street - 153
Cardiff, Wales - 49
Carlise (now O'Connell) Bridge - 63, 71, 95, 98, 104, 153, 186
'Carte de Visit' - 162
Cast Iron - 183, 185, 186, 190, 192, 195, 201, 214
Catherdral of St. John - 121
Catholics - 162
Catholic Emancipation - 170
Catholic Emacipation - 162, 170
Celbridge, Co.Kildare - 120
Cashel, Archbishop of - 120
Chapelizod - 101
Caricatures - 104/105
Charlemont House, Parnell Square - 109
Charlemont House - 111
China - 195
Chinese Bridges - 190
Christ Church Cathedral - 98
Church Street tenements - 105
Citizens' Provisional Committee of the Municipal Art Gallery - 89
Civil War - 142
Clerke, Sir Clement - 34
Clare, Dr. David - 166
Clare Street, Dublin - 86
Clonmell House, Harcourt St. - 85
Clydesdale horses - 128

Cofferdams - 219
Colley, Dudley - 72
Colley, Dudley - 73, 74
Collinge, Declan - 81
Cuneo, Terence - 136/137
Coalbrookdale at night - 42/43
Coalbrookdale, England - 33, 39, 45, 49, 51, 53, 61, 67, 186, 187, 192, 195
Coalbrookdale Locomotive - 51
Coalbrookdale Company, Ironworks or Foundry - 38, 45, 64, 67, 158, 184, 185, 186
Coalbrookdale Foundry, Works Interior View - 36/37
Coalbrookdale, The Old Furnace - 52
Coalbrookdale Upper Works - 30/31
Coalbrookdale Top Works Foundry - 50/51
Coghill, Rhoda - 259
Commissioners for Improving and Preserving Dublin Port - 64, 184
Connor, M - 65
Corrigan, William - 97
Courtney, Stephens & Bailey Foundry, Dublin - 201
Croppies Acre - 156
Crossing the Bridge - 72
Crow Street Theatre - 64, 158
Cosgrave, W.T - 107
'Cubists' - 98
Curvilinear Range Building Botanic Gardens, Glasnevin - 197
Custom's House - 98, 142, 169

Daly, Liam - 226
Dame Street, Dublin - 86
Darby, Abraham I - 33, 34, 38, 192
Darby, Abraham II - 33, 39, 41
Darby, Abraham III - 33, 41, 192
Darby, Rebecca - 45
Darby, Sarah - 45
Dawson Street, Dublin - 86
Deane, Thomas Manley - 86
Dearman, Richard - 45
de Courcy, Prof. John W. - 187

Dickinson, Barnard - 45
de Loutherbourg, Philip - 42/43
Dickinson, Barnard - 45
Dowlais, South Wales - 49
Drogheda - 123
Dublin - 63, 66, 67, 73, 85, 89, 95, 98, 101, 105, 109, 123, 128, 131, 138, 139, 141, 145, 156, 162, 164, 183, 186, 201, 205, 213, 214, 231
Dubliners - 73, 75, 77, 95, 153, 155, 156, 166, 169, 73, 175
Dublin & Drogheda Railway Co. - 195
Dublin, Bird's Eye View - 26/27
Dublin Castle - 71, 153
Dublin City Council - 25, 77, 205
Dublin City Council Images
Liffey looking East - 6/7
Ha'penny Bridge - 10/11
The Bridge, 1950s - 22
Georgian Dublin - 58/59
Wellington Bridge - 65
On the bridge 1980 - 66
On the bridge 2013 - 66
Dublin 1953 - 68/69
Bridge Adverts - 71
Bridge Adverts - 89
Acordian Player - 152
Early bridge image - 155
Dublin 1966 - 157
Liffey Swim - 162
Emancipation - 170
Hector Grey's - 174
Dublin 1974 - 176/177
Wraps come off - 180/181
Wooden Deck - 187
Bailey Bridge - 192
Skeleton Arch - 193
Arch Painting - 196
Entrance Railings - 200
Aerial View - 200
It's not art - 202
Railing Detail - 202
Underneath bridge - 203
Days of Sail 1813 - 260/261
Dublin City Gallery, The Hugh Lane - 73, 111
Dublin Coach Tours Poster - 156
Dublin Corporation - 23, 63, 64, 71, 73, 75, 86, 89, 90, 95, 97, 98, 100, 104, 105, 107, 166, 169, 170, 184, 201

Dublin in the days of sail 1813 - 260/261
Dublin Map - 170/171
Dublin Municipal Gallery - 90
Dublin Port - 135, 143
Dublin Quays 1973 - 176/177
Dublin Zoo - 105
'Duff' (Coal) - 143
Durand-Ruel, Paul - 86
Durham, England - 49

Easter Rising 1916 - 169
Emmet, Robert - 156
England - 158
Enterprise Ireland - 205
Espinasse, Captain - 123
Essex (now Grattan) Bridge - 64, 67, 95, 97, 153, 184
Euston, London - 53
Europe - 101, 195, 197
European Union Cultural Heritage, Europe Nostra Award - 77, 205

Farren, David - 18/19
Fibre Optic lighting - 228
First World War - 138
Ford, Richard - 39
For John Huston... - 167
Four Courts - 142, 155, 169
Fox, Shadrach - 34
French's Epilepsy Remedy - 166
French Revolution - 195
Friel, William - 95, 98
Fry's Chocolate - 173
'Futurists' - 98

Gallery of Modern Art - 85, 86, 107
General Post Office - 67, 169
Geoghegan, Samuel - 134
Georgian - 158, 162, 183
Gilroy, John - 135, 141, 145
Glamorganshire Canal - 49
Gogarty, Oliver St. John - 115
Government Buildings - 86
Gorman, Patrick - 205
Grattan Bridge - 155, 166, 219
Grand Canal - 131, 135
Greenpatch, Poolbeg - 67
Grey, Hector - 75, 173
Grey, Mary - 99

Note As 'The Ha'penny Bridge' appears on virtually every page in text, captions and/or images and due to space restrictions it has been omitted from this index. Artists who featured the bridge in their work however are listed under *Ha'penny Bridge* along with their names which are listed separately.

Griffin, Kevin - 144
Great Famine - 162
Greece - 190
Guinness - 124, 128, 131, 133, 135, 139, 141, 142, 143, 144
Guinness Advertising
  Porter - 123
  Smiling Pint - 124
  Toucan with bottle - 135
  Seals in zoo - 141
  Toucans in flight - 144/145
Guinness, Arthur Portrait - 118
Guinness, Arthur - 119, 120, 121, 123, 124
Guinness Barges
  Heading home - 116/117
  Castleknock - 126/127
  Under the Bridge - 129
  Filming Dublin - 133
  Victoria Quay - 134
  Loading barges - 136/137
  Passing under - 138
  Model of barge - 139
  Going downriver - 264/265
Guinness Barges - 98, 138, 143, 170
  Castleknock - 142
  Foyle - 138
  Dodder - 138
  Fairyhouse - 143
  Killiney - 142
  Lagan - 138
  Liffey - 138
  Moy - 138
  Sandyford - 142
  Shannon - 138
  Tolka - 138
Guinness 'Farmleigh' Barges - 142
Guinness 'Lighters' (barges) - 141, 144
Guinness Bottles - 122, 128
Guinness Brewery - 140
Guinness Captain - 120
Guinness Diesel Locos - 135
Guinness Fleet Flag - 126
Guinness Fleet (Sea) - 139
Guinness Harps - 143
Guinness Harps - 142, 143
Guinness Horses - 128, 133
Guinness Horses
  Horse's Brass - 131
  Loading Floats - 131
Guinness Labels - 132, 142
Guinness Lease - 121
Guinness Lease - 123
Guinness Brewery - 140
Guinness Brewery, Park Royal UK - 143

Guinness Lease - 121
Guinness, Richard - 120
Guinness Ships
  Miranda Guinness - 139
  Lady Patricia - 139
  W.M. Barkley - 139
Guinness 'Upper & Lower Levels' - 133, 134, 135,
Guinness Narrow Gauge Railway - 133, 141
Guinness Signs - 119, 138
Guinness Steam Engines - 134
Guinness Tanker - 144
Gunning, Jenny - 44

Half Penny Coin - 10, 67
Ha'penny Bridge - 62
Ha'penny Bridge - 70
Ha'penny Bridge - 74
Ha'penny Bridge, Dublin - 75
Ha'penny Bridge - 94
Ha'penny for your thoughts - 99
Ha'penny Bridge - View from the Grand Central - 125
Halfpenny Bridge - 154
Ha'penny Bridge Marketing Products - 164/165
Ha'penny Bridge - 184
Ha'penny Bridge leading to Batchelors Walk - 190/191
Ha'penny Bridge - 194
Ha'penny Bridge - 204
Ha'penny Bridge - 208
Hallett, John - 54/55
Hammersmith Works, Dublin - 197
Harding, James D - 49
Harland & Wolff - 138, 205
Harcourt Street Gallery - 105
Harrison, Sarah Cecilia - 104, 105, 107
Harrods, London - 173
Heaney, Liing - 204
Hector Grey's Shop - 174
Henry Street, Dublin - 86
Hetton, England - 49
Hetton Colliery Co. Durham - 49
Hibernia - 10, 67
Hillen, Sean - 100
'Hogs Head' (measure) - 138, 143
Home Rule - 109
Homage to Sir Hugh Lane Painting - 91

Homage to Sir Hugh Lane Detail of painting - 108
Hone, Nathaniel - 85
Hornor, Thomas - 46
'Hugh Lane: 100 Years' Exhibition - 111
Hugh Lane Gallery - 82/83, 84, 86, 88, 89, 90, 91, 92/93, 95, 96, 97, 98, 101, 104/105, 106, 107, 108, 109, 110
Hugh Lane Gallery interior Interior- 106
Hughes Contracts - 205
Hutchinson Poe, Colonel - 91, 111
Hyde, Siobhan - 208

Industrial Revolution - 25, 162, 195
Ireland - 123, 144, 158
Irish Architect, The - 107
Irishenco Construction - 205
Irish Free State - 109
Irish Free State Army - 142
Irish Independent - 98
Irish Parliament - 156
Irish rivers - 138
Irish Times - 73, 90, 97, 100, 107, 166
Iron & Steel Trades Confederation - 46
Ironbridge - 192
Ironbridge - 41
Ironbridge - 44
Ironbridge Today - 54/55
Ironbridge, Eye Patch Box - 33
Ironbridge, Porcelain Mug - 45
Iron Bridge - 39, 41, 45, 185, 187, 192
Iron Bridge (Dublin) - 158
Ironbridge Gorge - 33, 41
Ironbridge Gorge Trust Museum - 53
Iron Bridge Trade Token - 41
Ironmaking Blast Furnace Illustration - 47

James I, King - 34
James's Street, Dublin - 128, 133, 134
Johannesburg Art Gallery - 89
Johnston, Francis - 64, 184
Joyce, James - 158

Kearney, Peadar - 179

Keating, Sean - 91, 108
Keating, Sean - 109, 111
Kelly, Thomas - 91, 111
Kildare Street, Dublin - 86
Kildrought Brewery - 120
King's Bridge (now Heuston) - 183, 197

Lady Patricia (Ship) - 139
Lane, Sir Hugh - 84, 91, 104
Lane, Sir Hugh - 71, 73, 85, 95, 98, 100, 105, 107, 109, 111, 170
Lane Bequest - 111
Larkin, Jim - 100
LED Lighting - 228
Leixlip, Co.Kildare - 120, 123
Liffey Boardwalk - 114, 146/147
Liffey Boardwalk - 113
Liffey Bridge - 71, 169
Liffey Bridges - 226
Millennium Bridge installation - 221
Liffey Dockyard, (Vickers) - 142
Liffey Ferries - 63, 158, 183
Liffey, River - 97, 104, 120, 128, 133, 135, 141, 144, 145, 153, 183, 213
Liffey Street - 75
Lighting (Bridge) - 228
Lilleshall Company - 45
Limerick - 63
Lindsey House, London - 89
Lipstein, Daniel - 125
Liverpool - 139
Liverpool & Manchester Railway - 53
'Lockout', The - 105
Loop Line Railway Bridge, Dublin - 201
London - 49, 109, 156
London Brewers - 124
London Porters - 124
London Bridge - 63
London Bridge - 63
London & Birmingham Railway - 53
Lord Mayor of Dublin - 63, 123
Love Locks - 25
Love Locks - 168
LUAS Trams - 231
Lutyens, Sir Edwin - 71, 85, 89, 98, 104, 107, 111, 170
Lutyens, Sir Edwin - 86
Lusitania - 73, 109

Lyons, France - 192

Madeley Wood Furnaces - 34
Madeley Wood Furnaces - 34
Magnet of Poverty - 172, 173
Mallets Foundry, Dublin - 201
Mancini, Antonio - 84
Manet, Édouard - 86
Manchester - 139
Mansion House, Dublin - 89, 104, 105
Mansion House Committee - 95, 104, 107
MacDonaill, Dara - 172
MacGowan, Niamh - 190/191
McCann, Donal - 167
McCarthy, Desmond - 62, 201
McGowan, Rose - Cover, 194
MacPolin, Donal - 76
Matthews, Francis - 102/103
Mee, Giles - 123
Merchants Arch from the Ha'penny Bridge - 201
Merthyr Tydfil, Wales - 46, 49
Merthyr Tydfil, Ironworks - 46
'Metalock' Process - 201
Merrion Street, Upper - 71
Merrion Square, Dublin - 86, 101
Metal Bridge - 71, 73, 85, 86, 97, 98, 104, 158, 162, 184
Metropolitan School of Art - 86
Millennium - 219
Millennium Bridge - 213, 214, 220, 222, 226, 227, 228, 229, 231
Millennium Bridge, The - 230
Millennium Bridge Elevation - 214, 218/219
Millennium Bridge installation - 221
Millennium Bridge Plan - 222
Millennium Bridge Railings Elevation - 224
Millennium Bridge Abutment Elevation - 225
Monet, Claude - 86
Morisot, Berthe - 86
Morris, William - 231
Moore, Alan Jude - 209
Moore, George - 101

Mott McDonald EPO - 205
Municipal Art Gallery - 107
Municipal Gallery
   of Modern Art - 85, 90,
   105, 111
*Municipal Gallery of
   Modern Art - Impression
   - 82/83*
*Municipal Gallery of
   Modern Art - St. Stephen's
   Green - Impression - 88*
*Municipal Gallery of
   Modern Art - from
   O'Connell Bridge - 96*
*Municipal Gallery of
   Modern Art - alternate
   design - Plan & view - 97*
*Municipal Gallery of
   Modern Art - downriver
   Impression - 98*
*Municipal Gallery of
   Modern Art - from the
   quays - Impression - 101*
Murphy, William Martin
   - 90, 98, 100, 104, 105
Mycenean stone - 190

National Gallery of Ireland
   - 86, 90, 109
National Gallery, London
   - 73, 109, 111
National Library of Ireland
   - 169
Neil, James Crawford - 169
Nelson's Pillar - 75, 104
New York - 109
Nicholson, Francis - 35, 45
Nitrogen - 124
*No Evidence near the
   Ha'penny Bridge - 100*

O'Brien, Dermod
   - 90, 91, 111
O'Broin, Liam - 75
O'Carroll, Helen - 184
Office of Public Works
   - 95, 197
O'Connell Bridge - 23, 77,
   91, 111, 153, 166, 169, 231
O'Connell, Daniel - 162
O'Connell Street - 75
O'Connor, Niall - 29
Ó Direáin, Mártin - 81
Ogden, Perry - 92/93
Old Bridge (Fr.Mathew)
   - 155
Ordnance Survey Map of
   Dublin - 71
Ormonde Bridge - 155
Ormond Quay, Lower

- 77, 213
O'Rourke, Horace - 107
Orpen, Richard - 91, 111

Paine, Thomas - 195
Palais Egremont, Brussels
   - 77
Palm House, Belfast - 197
Palm House, Great
   (Kew, London) - 197
Paris - 197
Parkgate Street - 197
Parliament, Act of - 89
Parnell Square - 111
*Pearson, Peter
   - 163, 221, 230*
Percheron horses - 128
Penney, David - 47
Penydarren Ironworks - 46
Phoenix Ironworks, Dublin
   - 197
*Poems -
   In the City - 259
   The Halfpenny Bridge - 29
   Liffey Swim - 235
   Perversion at the Winding
   Stair Bookshop & Cafe - 209
   Ha'penny Bridge - 179
   Down by the Liffeyside
   - 179
   Liffey Bridge - 115
   Ill-mannered seagull - 81
   Dublin Jack of All Trades
   - 57
   In the City - 259*
Porter (beer) - 123
Portland Street - 128
Power, Albert - 111
Preston, England - 138
Price, Arthur - 120
Price & Myres - 215
Prime Minister of Gt.Britain
   - 158
Pritchard, Thomas - 192
Protestant - 63, 120
Purser, Sarah - 85, 111

Quakers - 41, 45

Rainbow Bridge - 169, 175
Rainsford, Sir Mark - 123
Rainsford, Mark II - 123
Rainsford's Beer - 123
Rathbone, Mary - 45
Renaissance Italy - 95
Renoir, Pierre-August - 86
Reynolds, Frank - 104/105

Reynolds, Frank - 105
Richmond Bridge
   (O'Donovan Rossa) -155
Richmond Tower - 155
'Rights of Man' - 195
River Liffey - 130
*River Liffey from Liberty Hall
   - 163*
Robertson, G - 32
Rock of Cashel - 120
Rodin, Auguste - 101
Rogers, Sarah - 94
'Romance in Ireland' - 107
Romans, The - 190
Rosie Hackett Bridge - 231
Ross & Walpole - 138
Roughan & O'Donovan - 231
Royal Barracks (now Collins)
   - 155
Royal College of Science
   for Ireland - 86
Royal College of Surgeons
   - 89
Royal Exchange (City Hall)
   - 153
Royal Hibernian Academy
   - 86
Russell, George - 91, 111

Sackville (O'Connell) St. - 95
Saint James's - 123
Saint James's Gate
   - 119, 120, 123, 124
Saint Patrick's Day - 155
Saint Stephen's Green
   - 89, 95
Salopian Journal - 64
Salopian Journal Notes - 64
Second World War - 135
Semple, John - 64, 184
Semple, George - 64, 153
'September 1913' - 108
Sargent, John Singer
   - 91, 111
Saturday Herald - 104
Severn Foundry, Dale End
   - 39
*Severn Foundry, Dale End
   - 39*
Severn, River - 33, 41, 186,
   192
Severn Gorge - 34
Smythe, Warrington - 34, 46
Skelton, John - 159
Shannon, River - 131
Sherlock, Lorcan - 89
Sheriff Street - 195, 197
Shifnal, England - 45

Shoneens - 63
Shropshire Coalfield - 45
Shropshire, England - 33, 45,
   67, 184, 185, 192
*Smelting House, Broseley
   - 32*
Smiles, Samuel - 192
Snedshill, England - 35, 45
Snedshill Ironworks - 35
Somonos, Juan Bosco - 8/9
South Wales - 46, 49
Spiker, Samuel Heinrich - 45
Spire, The - 75
Spratts Patent Dog Cakes
   - 173
Spreadwaters - 220
Staats Forbes Collection - 85
Stephenson, George - 49
Stone, Martin - 154
Stress Test Diagram - 196
Sunderland, England - 49
Sunderland Bridge - 49
*Sunderland Bridge, Plaque
   - 48*

Temple Bar - 86
Telford, Thomas
   - 45, 61, 192, 195
Timber Decking - 186
Timeline Chart - 20/21
Toll Booth - 73
Top Works Foundry - 51
Top Works Foundry - 50/51
Town Planning & Housing
   Association - 104
Traynor, Jessica - 235
Trevithick, Richard - 51
Trevithick's Locomotive - 51
Triangle Bridge
   - 71, 156, 158
Trout, Mr. - 175
Truss (Steel) - 215, 218, 220,
   228, 229
Turner, Richard - 197
Tyne & Wear rivers - 49

Uffizi Gallery, Florence - 71
Ulysses - 158
Under the Bridge - 203
United Kingdom - 107
United States of America
   - 95, 109, 195

Vibe for Philo, Poster - 166
Victoria Quay - 135, 141,
   142, 143, 144

Vivares, Francis - 30/31, 39
*View from Grattan Bridge
   - 76*

*Walcot, William - 82/83, 88,
   96, 98, 101*
Walcot, William - 98, 111
Walsh, William
   - 63, 64, 183, 184
War of Independence - 141
Waterloo, Battle of
   - 67, 71, 158, 185
Wellesley, Sir Arthur
   - 71, 158
*Wellington Bridge, The
   - 58/59, 65*
Wellington Bridge, Dublin
   - 45, 63, 67, 71, 158, 169
Wellington, Duke of
   - 67, 71, 158
Wellington Quay - 213
West Britons - 63
Williams, William - 40, 41
Wilkinson, John - 41, 45
Windsor, John - 45, 64, 67
Wood, J.G - 46
World War II - 143
*Workhouse Visual
   Communications - 28*
*Wraps come off, The
   - 180/181*

Yeats, John Butler - 95
Yeats, W.B - 90, 91, 98, 107,
   111

Zier, Kasper - 70